Val & Mick.

20.7.96

Many Happy Days ahead
we hope!

John & Zoë

xx

Table Decoration

Table Decoration

PAMELA WESTLAND

APPLE

A QUINTET BOOK

Published by The Apple Press
6 Blundell Street
London N7 9BH

ISBN 1-85076-510-3

Reprinted 1996

This book was designed and produced by
Quintet Publishing Limited
6 Blundell Street
London N7 9BH

Creative Director: Richard Dewing
Designer: Ian Hunt
Senior Editor: Laura Sandelson
Editor: Lydia Darbyshire
Photographer: Nelson Hargreaves

Typeset in Great Britain by
Central Southern Typesetters, Eastbourne
Manufactured in Singapore by Bright Arts Pte. Ltd.
Printed in Singapore by
Star Standard Industries Pte. Ltd.

Contents

Every time you arrange a table you have the opportunity to put into practice a wide range of artistic skills. Whether you are setting out places for a leisurely meal with your family and friends or for a formal dinner party, a celebration buffet or an alfresco meal in the garden, you can enhance the pleasure of the occasion by the setting you create.

Whether your principal tableware is white or brown, blue or gold, green or many coloured, you can use it to compose both high-fashion and low-key settings by your choice of accessories and decorations. Think of your tablecloths and place mats, table napkins and cutlery as a kaleidoscope – you can mix and match, blend and alternate colours and textures so that a basic set of plates and dishes takes on one new personality after another.

The later chapters, each one focusing on a different colour of dinnerware, have ideas galore for unusual table coverings and impromptu place mats, for napkin rings with style and individuality and table decorations that will rightly be the centre of admiring attention. Whether you are serving soup and sandwiches or a five-course meal this book is packed with inspirational ideas and clearly illustrated projects that will help you maximize your own artistic potential.

Introduction

PART  ONE

A crisp, white damask tablecloth set with gleaming silver,

sparkling glass and starched napkins as shapely as arum lilies; a

scrubbed pine table arranged with ivy green pottery, a posy of

bright marigolds and napkins casually tied in knots; a pretty tea

table, ringed with a garland of dainty summer flowers and set

with floral-patterned china, a jug of roses and lacy napkins; or a

zany setting of gold paper plates, black paper serviettes and

glitzy accessories – however formal or informal, carefully

planned or impromptu the meal, it is the style and ideas that will

ensure that your table setting rises to the occasion.

1   Setting the Scene

IN AN IDEAL WORLD perhaps we would all have a set of tableware for best, for everyday, for fun and for picnics. It is just possible, however, that the more limited one's resources, the more incentive there is to think creatively, to allow the imagination free rein and to compose a table setting that will rival the meal itself in terms of the guests' pleasure and enjoyment.

Arranging a table is, in about equal measure, a means of setting the scene for the meal and of making a personal statement – a way to express your own style, tastes and personality and even your mood. Just as you would not beg, borrow or hire a full complement of table silver and crystal if you were asking friends to come for a bowl of spaghetti, so it would be unwise to set a table with an exuberant cacophony of clashing colours if your own image tends to be one of restraint or reserve. There is a sad but true tale of an exceptionally elegant hostess, known for her extravagant chiffon gowns, who bequeathed all her purple and pink lace table linen to her niece. The poor young girl never gave a successful dinner party again; not until, that is, she had packed it all in a suitcase and taken it to a charity shop!

BELOW: A shallow basket of dried flowers, arranged to match your tableware, is ready to become the centre of attention, however impromptu the occasion. This decoration includes deep and pale pink peonies, strawflowers, lady's mantle, hydrangea and marjoram.

CHOOSING A STYLE

The colour and type of your tableware do not, by themselves, determine whether the setting will be formal or informal. What matters more in defining the style and mood of the setting are the accessories and utensils you decide to use together. Fine bone china alone does not make a setting formal or even elegant. Partnered with the appropriate cloth or place mats, napkins and cutlery such china can look stylishly upmarket. Teamed with, say, a coloured hessian tablecloth, matching napkins and a centrepiece arrangement of vegetables, the same china could look homely and casual, making a perfect setting for a gathering of family and friends. The later chapters, in which a variety of styles of tableware are mixed and matched with different table coverings and decorations, illustrate this point.

TABLECLOTHS

The choice between using a tablecloth or place mats is not necessarily one of convention or degree of formality, but of personal preference and expediency. If you are the proud owner of a highly polished dining table that is the centre of attention in your room, you may not care to hide it under an all-enveloping cloth. On the other hand, if the only table large enough for the occasion has a somewhat utilitarian appearance, you can give it a stylish lift by spreading it with a cloth chosen to match the mood of the moment. Similarly, the matter of colour and tone may come into your assessment. If, for example, the table is of the darkest polished oak and you want to present a light, bright and summery meal, a pretty floral or lace cloth may make this scene easier to create than the use of place mats, which would leave an uncovered expanse of uncompromising near-blackness.

Using a tablecloth makes it easier to achieve a unified look, because it provides a continuous background against which you can arrange the necessities for dining and the decorations, and it is especially beneficial when you have a large number of guests to seat and space is of the essence. With a tablecloth in place it is somehow easier to place the cutlery and glasses close together in such a way that no one notices the economy of space. When it comes to pushing place mats so closely together that they touch

LEFT: The crispness of the printed paper ribbon tied around a pile of embroidered table napkins or formed into a ring around a pretty lace napkin equals that of the table linen. A large ivy-patterned jug could be filled with a cascade of slender willow leaves and smaller jugs arranged with pale pink and apricot-coloured carnations.

or even overlap, however, the lack of elbow-room can be all too evident.

For a formal occasion, a white or faintly coloured damask tablecloth is the traditional, even the conventional table covering, but it is by no means the only option. If you do have such a cloth, perhaps one that has been handed down from another generation, you will know that, as long as it is immaculately laundered, it does have a certain style. It is something to do with the weight of the cotton and the way it drapes over the table corners; something to do with the subtle sheen in the weave and the way it adds to the sparkling effect of the cutlery and glasses; and, if the cloth is a family heirloom, something to do with the continuity and even nostalgia. Because not everyone lives close to a laundry or has the time or the inclination to launder damask cloths in the way they need – which includes thorough starching – high

quality tablecloths of this type can often be found at bargain prices in charity shops. They may be stylish just the way they are; they may need gentle bleaching to remove the mellowed look of age; or they may be the perfect candidates for a make-over project. When they are dyed black, bright red or rich, dark green, damask tablecloths take on a new look and set a completely new style.

The household linen departments of most large stores offer a wide selection of alternative options for formal dining, ranging from heavy, basket-weave cotton tablecloths to light, openwork ones, from exquisite handmade lace cloths (always an expensive choice) to cotton mixtures, which keep laundry fatigue to a minimum. But there are other more innovative choices, too. You can buy a length of furnishing fabric, with enough to make matching napkins if you wish, and simply machine or hand stitch the edges. White,

RIGHT: Stylishly wrapped table presents give the setting an extravagant air. Choose gold foil and gold paper wrappings or decorate tissue paper with gold stars and braid or spatter-sprayed gold paint. As for the trimmings, anything goes, as long as it's gold – the napkin ring, for example, is a band of embroidered braid.

cream or pastel-coloured broderie anglaise is a versatile choice, which can be used to set the scene for lunch, tea or dinner. To ring the changes or perhaps to echo one of the colours in the tableware, you can set the cloth over a coloured underlay. This can be an inexpensive (but washable) material that would show pink, green, coral-pink or whatever through the cut-work pattern to create an effect of coloured flowers. An equally versatile choice, and one that also has an air of formality, is an inexpensive machine-made lace bedspread, which can be laid directly on the table, or, for a more colourful effect, over a plain coloured underlay.

Heavy Indian cotton material with a thick self-coloured stripe is less formal than damask, cut-work or lace but is practical and stylish, and it looks especially effective with plain, modern pottery. You can buy it by the metre/yard in fabric departments or as a cotton "throw" – a single bedspread is large enough to cover a larger than average dining table. Look for these "throws" in dark and muted shades of navy, rust, bottle green and jade as well as in unbleached cream.

Printed cottons or cotton-mixture fabrics can be used for a multitude of theme creations. Jewel-bright paisley prints from India and bright-sun-and-blue-sky ones from Provence are rich canvasses on which to arrange bold shapes and plain colours, but it takes more than a skilled eye to achieve a successful pattern mix with assertive designs like these.

Bold flower patterns and small spriggy designs are at the opposite ends of the spectrum of printed floral fabrics, prettiest for an informal lunch or a leisurely tea-time occasion. Used sparingly or carefully colour-coordinated, bold stripes and coin-sized spots have a fresh, modern look for lunch or dinner settings. Colour-match one of the fabric shades to the principal colour of the tableware for a look of complete harmony.

If the occasion arises and you feel in the mood to put on a party, yet your table coverings look all too familiar, look beyond purpose-made cloths and lengths of fabric for the answer. Make it casual by teaming an eye-catching gift-wrapping paper with your boldest tableware, or use a frankly throw-away substitute, such

RIGHT: Spatter-patterned plates in rainbow colours have been teamed with a brightly printed table covering. The deep purple iris motif is brought to life with fresh flowers placed on the table, and the napkins are tied with a few wisps of ostrich feathers.

as wallpaper. Our choice, which you can see in Chapter 4, was for a bold purple and bottle green striped gift-wrap teamed with plain green disposable plates – perfect for an informal buffet, an outdoor meal or a children's party. You could add purple or green serviettes, a jamjar of purple anemones, pansies and marjoram flowers and – making sure that you keep them well above the paper covering – a cluster of candles in the two shades. At the end of the meal, when the guests have marvelled at your ingenuity, you can neatly wrap the scraps and disposables in the paper cloths, as they do in Continental restaurants, and rejoice at the simplicity of it all.

PLACE MATS

Like tablecloths, place mats can match the mood of a variety of occasions, from a formal dinner party to a casual gathering of family and friends. Choose from crisply starched linen or heavy-weight cotton with a cut-thread pattern at the corners. When you want to put on a show, use hand-made lace, while for more casual occasions choose from coarse linen or cotton weaves, bold cotton prints or woven rushes.

To add a touch of individuality you could buy or make plain place mats and use fabric paints to create a stencilled design in one corner – a pineapple, a shell or a spray of ivy leaves, for example – and repeat it on matching or toning napkins. If you are artistic, you could paint a design of your own on plain place mats, perhaps echoing the style of the floral pattern on the

china or introducing a favourite family theme such as cats, birds or boats, or a monogram of your initials. To keep your hand-painted designs looking fresh for as long as possible, follow the laundry instructions supplied with the paints.

No matter how varied the range of place mats you can buy, it is always satisfying to create styles of your own, purpose-made to match your furnishings and using interesting materials in unusual ways. Blue and white striped mattress ticking, boldly striped and hard-wearing deck chair canvas or remnants of tapestry canvas would all make stylish place mats for use on a variety of occasions. You could make the mats as covers to slip over heat-resistant table mats – this is a good way of giving ones that have lost their appeal a second life – fastening them along one edge with Velcro. Alternatively, you could make place mats with built-in heat resistance by lining them with a pad of washable quilting, machine or hand stitched in place with criss-cross lines or in a traditional pattern.

Heat-resistant mats are both functional and decorative, and they may be used alone on all but the most formal occasions. A polished table set with stylish cutlery, gleaming glass, a bowl of fresh flowers and a set of protective table mats that coordinate with the colour of the furnishings creates a welcoming lunch-time scene.

BELOW: The black underplates frame the dinnerware, visually separating the white china from the textured tablecloth. The black table napkins with grey borders link the two extremes.

TABLE NAPKINS

Table napkins have come a long way since the days when they were considered purely functional articles, to be spread across the lap or tucked into the collar to protect the diner's clothing from spills.

Before they are put to use, they have a significant part to play in the design of the table setting and its colour theme. At their most casual, table napkins may be chosen, as flowers are, to contrast or harmonize with the colours of the other decorations – to provide, for example, a cool note of neutrality to a vibrant colour mix or colour highlights to a table set with brown, white or cream china. At their most casual, too, table napkins can be folded simply and presented as neat rectangles, squares or triangles, or pulled through a napkin ring and arranged with a twist or twirl.

More formally, table napkins of starched white or pastel-coloured linen or cotton can be fashioned into decorative shapes to resemble a water lily, a fan, a bishop's mitre and many other designs. Napkins folded into these fancy shapes – some of which are, happily, far less complicated to achieve than they seem – become the focus of admiration more for the neatness and ingenuity of the design than for the colour and texture of the articles themselves. Often a small gift, a flower, a place card or a pair of chopsticks is tucked into the folds of the napkin, and many of the popular styles were designed for this purpose.

The Cock's Comb

With its five upstanding points, this design looks more difficult to achieve than it is. It is particularly effective when coloured napkins are used.

1 Fold the napkin into four quarters, then fold it diagonally.

2 Place the napkin so that the points of the triangle are facing away from you. Fold over the two sides so that the edges meet vertically at the centre. Turn under the two points now facing you so that the shape is triangular again.

3 Fold the napkin in half along the centre line and stand it on edge with the folded side uppermost. Tuck one of the end flaps behind the other to secure the shape. Pull up each of the four pleats along the length and arrange them neatly.

The Bat

This aptly named fold, with its wide wingspan, can be presented in a wine glass or held at the base in a napkin ring.

1 Fold over the top one-third of the napkin, then fold under the lower one-third. You will have a narrow strip with one edge on top along the edge facing you. Turn up the two corners at each edge of the strip.

2 Fold the lower, folded edge upwards to make a 2.5cm/1in pleat along the length of the strip. Turn over a pleat 2.5cm/1in wide at one short edge of the strip, and pleat the napkin evenly along its length. Secure the winged shape at the base with a rubber band or with a piece of string if you are not ready to arrange it in a wine glass.

The Rose

This flower-shaped design, which has eight "petals", is an ideal way of presenting a small gift, a single flower, a posy or a bread roll to each guest.

1 Place the napkin flat. Fold the four corners into the centre, then fold the four "new" corners into the centre. Repeat this process once more.

2 Turn the napkin over and fold the four corners to the centre. Stand a plate or tumbler in the centre of the napkin to hold the points in place. Reach underneath the napkin and pull out each of the four corners to make the first row of petals.

3 Remove the plate or tumbler and, holding the centre points in place, reach between the raised petals and pull out the turned-over points to create four more. Ease the petals all round to make them even.

The Envelope

One of the simplest of napkin folds, this design is as effective
with linen or cotton napkins as with paper serviettes. It is
especially useful as a way of holding a place setting of cutlery or
a menu or place card.

1 Fold the napkin into four
quarters. Fold over the first
point so that it covers the centre
fold and the second and third
points at graduated levels.

2 Turn over the napkin and
fold over each of the two sides.
Run a finger along the folds to
hold them in place.

The Bishop's Mitre

This is a favourite design in hotels and restaurants, but achieving a perfect shape may take a little practice.

1 Begin by folding the napkin in half so that one long side is towards you. Fold both layers of the bottom left, and fold the top right corners so that the edges meet vertically at the centre. Turn the napkin over and fold it in half horizontally, along its length.

2 Pull out one point from the top of the napkin and another from underneath it. At this stage it will look like a long, low house with a pointed gable at each end.

3 Fold the napkin into three and tuck the point at one end deep between the layers of the point at the opposite end.

In Victorian times, when formal dining was the order of the day, representational designs had their heyday, and creations with names such as the princess, the waterfall and the lady's slipper graced the tables of the aspiring rich and famous. In *The Book of Household Management,* published in 1898, Mrs Beeton impressed upon her readers the care necessary then, as now, to present table napkins in such a way that they would enhance both the setting and the occasion.

> In ordinary family use they [table napkins] are sometimes folded smoothly and slipped through "napkin rings", made of bone, ivory or silver; in fact, after first using, this is generally the case, each member of the family having his or her own ring. But . . . those required for dinner-parties and other formal occasions should be neatly and prettily folded. . . . It must, however, be remembered that it is useless to attempt anything but the most simple forms unless the napkins have been slightly starched and smoothly ironed. In every case the folding must be exact, or the result will be slovenly and unsightly. A small dinner-roll . . . should be placed in each napkin . . . while, whenever it is possible to do so, the appearance of the dinner table will be greatly improved by putting a flower or small bouquet in each napkin.

Mrs Beeton's advice about the importance of starching and the neatness of the corners is still applicable today if formal designs are attempted. Luckily, however, the introduction of spray starch has lightened the laundry task and will give results that would, surely, have met with that author's approval. Trim corners are less easy to achieve, but it is a fact that a napkin that is not truly square to start with will not present neatly, however carefully it is folded.

Table napkins have become smaller since Victorian times, when it was recommended to use dinner napkins 75cm/30in square. Now the accepted size for dinner napkins, the ones most likely to be folded into classic or traditional shapes, is 65cm/26in square, and breakfast napkins, which can be used on all informal occasions, are usually 60cm/24in square. The step-by-step photographs show clearly how to achieve some of the most popular shapes for a formal dinner, while throughout the book the illustrations show that a less structured approach can add immeasurably to the visual effect of a table setting.

The range of materials considered suitable for napkin rings has been greatly extended since the turn of the century – indeed, this sphere of table decoration offers some of the greatest scope for imagination and creative thinking. Bone, ivory and silver napkin rings always look remarkably stylish, and if you have such a set, perhaps one that is a family heirloom, you will find a number of ideas later in the book to help you to use napkin and napkin ring in a number of fresh ways. If you want to present the napkin ring in the centre of the napkin, you can arrange the material in a neat roll or a flat pack, in the shape of a bow or as a loosely folded letter S. You can hold the napkin by the point in the centre, shake it to form a loose triangle and push just the narrow point through the ring. You can fold the napkin to make a perfect triangle and slip the corner into the ring in a similar way, or you could roll the napkin into a tight tube and slip the ring close to one end. This asymmetrical presentation is most effective when the napkin ring is particularly eye-catching – when, for example, it is an exuberant bow of gold lamé or gossamer ribbon, a hoop of flowers or berries, or a band of richly embroidered braid.

CUTLERY

Perhaps the most important observation to make about cutlery is that it should be polished until it shines. Whether it is made of silver, silver plate or stainless steel, the gleam and glisten of polished cutlery can contribute significantly to the appearance of a table setting. Keep a clean, dry, soft cloth alongside the cutlery in a drawer to give it a final shine, as certainly happened in Mrs Beeton's day.

Cutlery with plastic handles in red, green, blue, black, cream and other colours is indispensable for everyday use, outdoor eating and picnics and, if it is carefully chosen, will form a coordinated part of your overall theme. If you cannot indulge in the luxury of a number of sets, choose a colour that best complements your most frequently used tableware. Knives and forks with cream handles, for example, look well with brown, cream and yellow china or pottery, while cutlery with navy blue handles looks stylish with blue and white, dark green and red and white china.

If you are planning to buy a set of cutlery for special occasions think carefully before making your decision. You may have modern furniture and furnishings now, but will that always be the case? Is it possible that you will later turn to more traditional styles? Is your present tableware likely to endure as your primary set, or will it be superseded later, as finances allow? The partnership between cutlery and tableware is an important one – after all, the knives and forks, dishes and plates are destined to spend every special occasion in close proximity, so it is up to you to ensure that they do so in perfect harmony! If possible, take a plate or bowl from your tableware with you when you are choosing the cutlery or ask the cutlery supplier for a sample piece so that you can arrange it with your china. Some cutlers offer this as a standard part of their service, so that you can judge for yourself at home whether, for example, it is the king's pattern or a fiddle and thread design that will most perfectly complement your table service.

Although there is a conventional way of arranging cutlery on formal occasions, it is up to you whether you adhere to it. It is customary for cutlery to be arranged in the order in which it is to be used, starting from the outside and working in. This convention has a practical advantage, because it allows guests to see how many courses are to be served and to pace themselves accordingly. In addition, even at the height of the most animated conversation, they can be sure of picking up the appropriate implements without thinking about it.

Arranging cutlery in this way does presuppose a generous amount of table space. For example, on the right of the plate and working outwards there might be a dessert spoon, a dinner knife, a fish knife or dessert knife (frequently now used in place of a fish knife), a soup spoon and another dessert knife to be used with bread and with the cheese course. Balancing this array, on the left of the plate and on the right of the bread plate, and again working outwards from the plate, there would be a dessert fork, a dinner fork and a fish fork or another dessert fork. Sometimes the dessert knife is placed on the bread plate on the left of the place setting; sometimes it is placed horizontally across the top of the dinner plate, with the handle pointing to the right.

If space from side to side is limited or if you want a less formal appearance, the dessert spoon and fork can be placed above the dinner plate, the spoon on top with the handle to the right and the fork below it, facing in the opposite direction. This arrangement is much more frequently used at family meals, when even an abbreviated version of the horizontal layout might seem unduly formal.

Other ways of displaying or presenting cutlery can bring a note of individuality to a table setting. You may like to tie each place setting of knives, forks and spoons into a bundle with paper ribbon, satin ribbon, gauze ribbon, shiny cord or an iris leaf and place it on the dinner plate. You could slip each person's complement of cutlery through a conventional napkin ring or, if the meal is alfresco and the cutlery is plastic, you could stand each group of cutlery upright in a bamboo ring.

Different occasions will prompt different solutions for table arrangements, and the way you present the cutlery will have its part to play in the overall effect. If, for example, you are serving tea to celebrate a baptism, you could add to the decorative effect of the table by tying the knives in bundles of six or eight with white, pink, blue or lemon-coloured satin ribbon. If the occasion was to celebrate a golden wedding, you could tie the cutlery with multiple twists of shiny gold cord, while for a Christmas buffet you could wrap each place setting of cutlery in a red or green napkin tied around with tartan ribbon.

The presentation of a Chinese, Japanese or Malaysian meal gives you the opportunity to create a different cultural ambience around the table, perhaps by using split cane place mats, decorative rice bowls and, if you are sure your guests have mastered the technique, chopsticks. Long, slender and elegant as they are, chopsticks lend themselves to a variety of decorative arrangements. You can fold a napkin tightly around them to make a neat, compact roll thin enough to push through a plain wooden napkin ring or you could tie it around with a few strands of raffia.

You can fold two opposite corners of a napkin to the centre to make a long thin strip of fabric and simply knot it around the centre of the chopsticks, or you could place the chopsticks on top of a napkin folded into a neat parcel and tie them around with a slender twig of willow, chives or iris leaves. Ribbons and bows are less appropriate to the presentation of oriental meals, but flowers add a pretty and authentic finishing touch. You can tuck a simple white or cream spray chrysanthemum or spider chrysanthemum (choose a small one, from a side shoot) into the napkin ring or under the leaf tie, or place a larger bloom, removed from its stem so that it lies facing fully upwards, on each dinner plate.

GLASSES

Sparkling glass, glinting in every shaft of sunlight or flicker of candlelight, will add the perfect finishing touch to a table setting, whatever the occasion. How much duller life would be if it were the custom to serve wine and water in earthenware beakers!

Choose a style of glasses that harmonizes with the tableware and cutlery. Although there are no hard and fast rules about what goes with what, it is easier to achieve a balanced look if the three major elements on the table – the glasses, the tableware and the cutlery – are all based on traditional designs or are all, by contrast, in a modern style.

Whether your choice is for the finest cut crystal, which has the highest sparkle factor, or for plain glass in any style, each type of vessel will have common elements that owe nothing to design and everything to practicality. You would not, for example, serve chilled white wine in a tumbler, because handling the glass would raise the temperature of the wine. Equally, and for the opposite reason, you would not serve brandy in a long-stemmed goblet, which would make it difficult to cradle the glass to warm the spirit and so release its aroma.

On formal occasions you may set one glass for white wine, one for red wine and one for water. If you plan to offer port, brandy or liqueurs at the end of the meal it is accepted that you will ask your guests their preference and set out the appropriate glasses as you bring in the tray of drinks.

White wine glasses, which are always on a long stem, may be of Paris goblet shape, with a round bowl, a tulip shape, which is more elongated and narrows at the top, or the flute or trumpet shape, which has straight sides broadening at the top. Coloured glasses, which are sold specifically for use with German and Alsatian wines, are not usually recommended by wine buffs, because they distort the colour of the wine.

Red wine glasses, which may be of either the Paris goblet or tulip shape, will also have stems, but in this case the purpose of the stems is to enable guests to swirl fine wines gently in the glass to release the bouquet.

If you plan to serve a single wine throughout the meal or to offer guests a choice of red or white wine, a goblet or a tulip-shaped glass would be appropriate.

LEFT: Regardless of quality or design, the shapes of drinking glasses have developed for practical reasons. Shown here, from left to right, back row: tall-stemmed hock glass; cut glass for red wine; trumpet-shaped white wine or champagne glass; Paris goblet for red or white wine. Centre row: port glass; tulip-shaped red wine glass; red or white wine glass; brandy balloon. Front row: cut crystal tumbler; waisted liqueur glass; cut glass for whisky and other spirits; cut crystal sherry glass; sherry copita.

If you are going to offer water or other non-alcoholic drinks you can use a tumbler or, on the principle that the less the glass is handled, the cooler the liquid will remain, any large glass on a stem.

The arrangement of glasses on the table follows a similar convention to that applied to cutlery. Glasses are placed above and to the right of the dinner plate and, working from the outside inwards, in the order in which they will be used. Thus you may position a water glass furthest from the plate, a white wine glass (to be used during the first course) next to it, followed by a red wine glass (if the main dish is appropriate to it) and, nearest the plate, a small glass for port if you plan to pass the decanter, always to the left, after the meal.

So much for formality, an array of glasses – and a formidable bill at the wine merchant's. As we all know, at a casual gathering when the conversation flows and the atmosphere is exhilarating, you can serve a modest wine in a tumbler and still get top marks for style.

If any course on the menu is to be eaten with the fingers, it is a thoughtful gesture to provide each person with a finger bowl. Guests who have enjoyed whole unshelled prawns, globe artichokes or asparagus

will appreciate this consideration and the opportunity to use an extra table napkin (it may be a paper one) as a hand towel. Finger bowls may be any china, glass or earthenware cereal, dessert or rice bowls; choose the prettiest ones you have. They are usually placed slightly above and to the left of the dinner plate, in order, it is said, to prevent absent-minded guests from mistaking them for a wine glass! Half-fill the bowls with warm water and, for appearance's sake, scatter a few rose petals on the surface, float a thin slice of lemon or lime or add a sprig of mint.

SEATING ARRANGEMENTS

A few minutes spent by the host or hostess with pencil and paper before guests arrive may make all the difference to the success of a meal. The question of who sits next to whom, which is a matter of etiquette on formal occasions, is no less important at a gathering of friends or extended family, and it is best not to leave it to chance or to a hasty decision made when everyone has converged on the table. While guests with shared interests may welcome the chance to be seated next to one another, it may be better to separate them during the meal if they are likely to indulge in an extended period of shop-talk, to the exclusion of their neighbours. Equally, if there is likely to be a clash of personalities, it is diplomatic to seat those concerned at a safe distance.

On formal occasions, it is usual for the host and hostess, if, indeed, there are both, to be seated at opposite ends of the table, and for guests to be seated, male and female alternately, along the sides. When there are six or ten in the group and the company is equally divided, this arrangement works well. But as anyone who has a rectangular table and has given a dinner party for eight knows, some other arrangement is needed. The answer is for either the host or the hostess to move one place around from the end of the table and for a senior guest to be asked to take that position. This situation does not arise, of course, when seating is planned for a round table, although it is still advisable for a host and hostess to sit on opposite sides so that they can attend to the needs of the guests seated close to them.

There are so many last-minute details to attend to just before serving a meal that it is a good idea to write out a table plan and to refer to it discreetly before you direct guests to their seats. That is much easier than causing them to play a game of musical chairs if, after all your best-laid plans, you inadvertently sit a petulant aunt next to her arch rival.

Another way is to write place cards for each guests and to position them in advance of the meal. In that way, no one, least of all the host or hostess, will be in any doubt where they are to sit. It may also overcome the murmur of embarrassment caused by a host who, unprepared to be displaced from his usual seat, said to a woman guest, "Hey, you're sitting in my chair!"

Place cards should be as fun or as formal as the rest of the table setting. You can buy inexpensive miniature picture frames or you could make suitable frames by covering cards with gift-wrapping paper or furnishing braid. If you are having a meal for a special occasion you can cut shapes from coloured card – a mask or a cat for Hallowe'en, a big golden sun for high summer and so on – and write or stencil the names on those. Or you can write the names on small flag shapes, stick them to split canes, bendy straws or chopsticks and tuck them into the table napkins.

For more formal occasions, when, for example, the "principal lady guest" would be seated on the host's right and the next in seniority on his left, you can buy china, glass or silver-plated stands with slots to hold the name card. These are placed just above the dinner plate or just above any cutlery that is in that position.

With the table beautifully arranged, everyone seated and the first course about to be served, guests may not be aware of how much forethought and preparation has gone into the setting that earns their delighted comments. And that is just as it should be.

ABOVE: Note the place cards with bird motif and matching colourful wooden birds on the napkins.

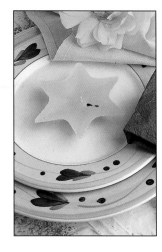

You may decide to fill a spare vegetable dish until it is overflowing with a cascade of hops and sweet peas; to create a ring of rosy apples and their leaves; or to float a handful of rose petals and a few colourful candles in a bowl of water. You might like to involve the family in creating paper decorations such as party crackers or in pressing flowers and leaves for later assembly into rings to surround the plates. Or you might like to flatter each guest with an individual arrangement of flowers and herbs or a take-home gift of flowers or bon-bons in a miniature carrier bag. Whatever your choice and whatever your style, the way you decorate the table will make your personal mark on the occasion just as surely as the meal you serve.

2 Table Decorations

FLOWER ARRANGEMENTS

Flowers have such a long association with celebrations of all kinds, with festivals and festivities, with social and family gatherings, that it is natural to think of them first when you are planning your table decorations. From a sparkling glass bowl of roses, which will take centre stage at a formal dinner, to a handful of vibrant blooms when you are hosting a barbecue in the garden, flowers can match the mood of any occasion and provide a powerful focal point.

Some species and some ways of arranging them are better suited to one ambience than another, although if a little thought is given to the relationship between the colours of the flowers, the container and the table setting, most perceived barriers can be crossed successfully. A jug of wayside poppies, which would be perfectly suited to a country-style setting and a scrubbed pine table, could look equally stunning in a modern environment with black place mats and napkins on a glass table. If, in this case, the container were black – a straight-sided glass or pottery vase, perhaps – the poppies would be as effective as, say, a trio of white lilies or a single rose.

The choice of container as much as the flowers and foliage sets the tone of an arrangement. If you want to achieve perfect harmony between your table setting and a floral decoration, you may be able to use a spare piece of the tableware as a container. A vegetable dish, soup tureen, sauce boat, matching teapot or a trio of cereal bowls could all be used, in their different ways, for a table arrangement. Even a piece of china that has become chipped can be given a second life in this way. A discreetly arranged trailing leaf or flower over the affected area will make the piece seem as good as new.

You can link the tableware with the container in other ways, too. You could select a flower holder that matches one of the principal colours in the china pattern or paint a not-too-valued container in a toning shade. If, for example, you are setting the table with gold-rimmed china and have pressed every piece into service, consider using a gold container. You may be able to use a gilt teapot or water jug, which would be ideal for full-blown roses or parrot tulips, or a brass plate or bowl. When the occasion has more dash than cash and the gold plates are paper, flowers would look fabulous in an empty food can sprayed with gold paint.

Functional and decorative items from around the home, many of them far removed from the conventional vases, make stylish flower holders that might also become a talking point around the table. A cluster of creamware jugs, each filled with a different kind of flower, creates a palette of artistic interest. A group of mugs or beakers filled with white marguerite daisies contrasts a multitude of colours and patterns with the neutrality of white flowers. An assortment of wine glasses holding miniature posies or supporting individual flowers looks well as a group or would be equally pleasing if one were allocated to each place setting. A collection of glass storage jars can look stylishly up-country when some are filled with dried beans and pasta and others with flowers. And, by contrast, some used scent bottles holding dainty flowers such as primroses, violets and forget-me-nots will make a delicate tea-time grouping.

BELOW: The clear blue and yellow pattern on the pottery gives a strong colour cue for the floral decorations. Each guest has a colour-matched gift bag of scented flowers or wrapped chocolates. Table napkins have been folded into gentle fan shapes and decorated with full-blown yellow roses.

UNUSUAL CONTAINERS

Hollow stems have a part to play in container groupings, too. Bamboo stems, sawn to graduated lengths but all perfectly level at the base, can be tied together in a bundle with raffia or string and used to display dried flowers and preserved leaves, the more dramatic the colouring the better. Individual bamboo stems can be used in a similar way, but three or four will have a greater impact. Stand the stems on a flat dish or plate, anchoring them with a little adhesive clay if necessary, and pile a handful of washed pebbles around them.

You can also use these stem vases to display fresh flowers, by inserting a small piece of soaked stem-holding foam into the top of each one or by placing an orchid phial or another slender water holder inside each stem. Because bamboo has such strong associations with the Far East, these natural vases look most effective when you adopt a minimalist approach to the flowers. You may like to display a stem of ice-green hellebore in one, a trio of spear-like leaves in another and a dramatic day lily in a third, or create an understated effect by using just three white or cream chrysanthemums.

Although they have less obvious decorative appeal, other dried and hollow stems – hogweed, hollyhock and cow parsnip, for example – can be given a similar kind of vase-life. Gather the stems into a bundle and stand them in a glass container such as a fish-bowl or crackle-glass vase, fit water-holding phials to the tops of some of the stems and fill them with bright wayside or garden flowers. Marigolds, anemones, zinnias, campions and poppies will all look more colourful in contrast with the textured stems.

Shells, too, have just the kind of texture to complement flowers. Formal settings can be enhanced by an arrangement of, say, cream and apricot-coloured roses and cream and pink ranunculus blooms arranged with a few wisps of light-coloured foliage in a large cone or conch shell. If your setting has a faintly maritime theme – you might be using ship's style knotted cotton place mats and napkin rings – you could arrange the shell with appropriately seashore flowers such as sea lavender and sea holly and use sprays of dried seaweed in place of foliage.

A problem that does arise when you arrange flowers in a shell, straw cornucopia or a vase placed, just to be different, on its side is that the arrangement is almost certain to have a "best side", and it may make those guests who are unable to enjoy that side feel, even jokingly, as if they had been placed "below the salt". One hostess, who was famed for her lavish table decorations, overcame this dilemma by giving the cornucopia a quarter-turn at intervals throughout the meal, so that each group of guests was able, in turn, to admire the carefully wired cascade of fruit and flowers. If you wouldn't feel comfortable doing that, try using two containers, placing them so that they face in opposite directions.

The point of view is an important consideration, no matter what type of container you use. Whether you are arranging flowers and foliage in a round bowl, a rectangular box, a wine flask or a basket, you must make sure that the decoration is equally attractive from every angle. Unless your table is placed against a wall or a screen, when the flower arrangement can be one sided, make sure that it is equally pleasing to guests all around the table. You do not need to go to the lengths of composing two opposing sides as negative images of each other, but there should be a more or less equal distribution of colour and feature flowers so that none of the guests has cause to feel disadvantaged.

ABOVE: The dried flower design, arranged in a dark blue stone pot, includes bleached and dyed eucalyptus leaves, sea lavender and red rosebuds. Blue and white tableware contrasts well with a rust-red paisley pattern tablecloth and plain, pleated napkins.

PRESSED FLOWER ARRANGEMENTS

One especially attractive way to ensure that your guests feel pampered is to surround each dinner plate, or the underplate on which it stands, with a ring of pressed leaves or flowers arranged as a collage. You can choose fallen woodland leaves and seed carriers in shades of nut brown, variegated leaves such as ivy or pineapple mint in soft green and cream, or a galaxy of garden flowers and petals, roses and pansies, peonies and primulas. If it is a large gathering and your reserves of pressed flowers are low, make a ring for one or two of the principal dishes – perhaps a circle of pansies to outline the foot of a pedestal cake-stand or a ring of woodland leaves to emphasize a rural theme. The materials and the method are shown in Chapter 6.

Pressed flowers and leaves can be used to make three-dimensional table decorations, too. These have the advantage of being long-lasting, ready whenever you have unexpected guests or time is not on your side. Preformed polystyrene shapes, which are aesthetically unpleasing in their undecorated state, can be used in a variety of ways to create some wonderful designs. You can cover the spheres with pressed leaves or flowers

and display them individually on small pedestal stands or pile three or four together in a shallow dish or basket. The cone shapes can be covered with overlapping leaves in differing shapes, sizes and colours to simulate trees, and the ring shapes can be covered first with pressed leaves to conceal the grey foam and then with a symmetrical or random arrangement of dried flower heads – bright pink or yellow strawflowers, for example.

The bay leaf ball illustrated above shows how effective these pressed flower decorations can be. Use a strong, all-purpose adhesive, start at the base and work upwards – you will soon see the design taking form. The finished arrangement, which bears a non-accidental resemblance to a globe artichoke, was brushed with gold craft powder to add sparkle to a party setting.

In a similar way you can decorate plain or dyed eggs with pressed flowers and display them in a group of coordinated eggcups; arranged on a bed of moss or hay in a basket or, if you happen to have one, in a long-abandoned birds' nest, and you need not confine this arrangement to Easter.

FRUIT AND VEGETABLES

Arrangements of fruits and vegetables can have just as much impact as a flower decoration. In fact, because they may be in an unfamiliar context they may be even more striking. It can be effective to combine fruit and flowers or vegetables and flowers in ways that draw attention to the colour, texture and visual appeal of the edible components.

For an informal, country-style lunch in the garden or on the terrace you could decorate the table with a shallow basket of vegetables – broccoli and sweetcorn, garlic and carrots, for example – and highlight the arrangement with a ribbon of brilliant flowers, such as marigolds, nasturtiums and pansies. Alternatively, you could arrange a basket of apples and pears and highlight some of them with a few sprays of clary or posies of clove-scented carnations.

For more formal compositions both fruit and vegetables can be mounted on wires and used with or instead of flowers in table arrangements. You could, for example, separate a small cauliflower and the heads of broccoli into florets, create false stems from stub wires (see Good Enough to Eat! in Chapter 6) and arrange them in stem-holding foam in a basket or glass bowl. Partnered with cream lilies or roses, green nicotiana and sprays of herbs, the vegetables can hold their own in any company.

Some fruits and vegetables can be used as flower containers, when their texture, shape and colour is a foil for a floral arrangement. Attractive and visually interesting fruits like melons, grapefruits and oranges, and vegetables, such as marrows and other squashes, can be hollowed out and the shells fitted with soaked, stem-holding foam. A watermelon shell, for example, could be filled with an arrangement of flowers in that characteristic vibrant sunset-red colour and, for contrast, mauve or dark blue. Ornamental cabbages, with their attractively frilled and variably coloured leaves, become all the more ornamental when they are decorated with flowers. Simply insert a selection of fresh flowers to nestle among the leaves. Choose flowers that will last well out of water, such as roses, carnations, spray carnations, spray chrysanthemums, marigolds and honeysuckle, and ones that will not, in design terms, be overpowered by the unusual presentation.

Continuing the vegetable theme, you could decorate a lunch or dinner table with a lettuce posy, made up of frilled lettuce leaves and bright garden flowers arranged in the hand and wired together. An example of this idea may be seen in Chapter 4. If you place this Victorian-style posy with a difference in a shallow bowl so that all the stems can reach the water, it should last for several days.

There is a long-established tradition of using floral designs in the round, and wreaths and rings have signified friendship, regard and welcome since pagan times. What better shape could there be for a centrepiece for your table? You can use preformed rings made of a variety of materials, all of which are available from florists and which can be reused on subsequent occasions. Rings made of twisted vine or clematis twigs or of supple willow may be decorated with vegetables, fruit, dried flowers and, for a short-term display, fresh flowers, too. Select the plant materials according to the style and mood of the occasion. Bunches of vegetables, such as green beans, spring onions, baby carrots, radishes, asparagus and herbs, will make a colourful display, high on texture and originality. A light spray of water – not so much that the drops spill on to the table-top – will give the decoration a fresh-as-the-morning-dew appearance.

On other occasions – Hallowe'en or Christmas, for example – it might be more appropriate to create a table ring of wired fruit. Small, rosy apples mounted on wires can be alternated with leaves on a twig ring or a preformed foam one; kumquats, as bright as sunshine, can be pierced with wooden cocktail sticks and pushed into the foam ring among sprays of evergreens to create an attractive decoration for the winter festivities; and mixed nuts, some spatter-sprayed with gold, can be stuck to a twig ring, where they will contrast effectively with its craggy texture.

For a summer gathering, an absorbent foam ring decorated with garden flowers, such as pansies, pinks, marigolds and mallow, will be the centre of attention when it is highlighted with a cluster of strawberries speared on cocktail sticks. Later in the year, a foam ring completely covered with sprays of blackberries at all stages of their development – blossom and ripening and ripe fruit – will look exquisite with the addition of a cluster of dark blue, red and purple tapers or a candle.

ABOVE: A casual meal or an informal drinks party in the garden calls for a relaxed approach to table decoration. The shallow garden trug contains an arrangement of a green cauliflower, heads of sweetcorn and gourds. Hidden blocks of soaked, stem-holding foam wrapped in foil provide a moisture source for the colourful band of cosmos, clary, nasturtiums and marigolds.

CANDLE DECORATIONS

The flicker of candlelight adds immeasurably to the atmosphere of a meal, whether it is a lunch party that lingers on until dusk, supper served in the garden at sunset or dinner at any time of the year at all. The light of the candles on the table draws the guests' concentration inwards and creates a greater feeling of intimacy and togetherness.

You may have three, four or five candlesticks all of a kind, crystal, brass or china ones, for example, which you could cluster together for maximum impact. On a formal occasion it might be appropriate to choose all the candles to match or to contrast strongly with the tableware. White or cream candles create a cool, elegant look, or you could use navy blue or burgundy red ones if they would echo one colour in the pattern on the china, or jade green ones to match the table napkins and reinforce a colour highlight chosen to contrast with, say, chestnut brown china.

For a less formal meal you might like to choose a range of colours. Pink, blue, green and yellow candles might each pick up a colour in a floral pattern on the dinnerware or be reflected in the choice of flower colours in the table arrangement. At a small gathering,

when it would not involve using a forest of a dozen or so candles, you could position a small candleholder, each with a different coloured candle, in front of each place setting, then, instead of having place cards, you could direct guests to the place setting with the blue candle, the green one and so on.

If you want to give a colour coordinated theme party or if you just do not have candlesticks that complement your tableware for a particular occasion, you can transform inexpensive ones with acrylic paints or spray paints. It is easy to paint unremarkable glass candlesticks of the type you might find in a charity shop and give them a verdigris-like finish. You can use the same technique with different colours to give glass, china, wooden or even plastic candlesticks a spattered finish. You could, if you prefer, paint the holders in a single colour and, when it is dry, sponge on another colour to give a ragged or dragged look. If you use water-soluble paint, the transformation can be a temporary design measure or you can have second, third or more colour thoughts as the whim takes you.

The combination of candles, flowers and foliage is always attractive and never more so than when a pedestal candlestick is adapted as a flower container. You can do this quite easily by fitting a purpose-made, plastic, dish-like attachment with a plug that fits into the candle aperture and that is just the right size to hold a block of stem-holding foam. Buy the dish and foam from a florist's shop. When it is in place and secured to the candlestick with adhesive tape, the holder can be filled with, for example, hops, fennel, spray carnations and roses, arranged around the central feature, which could be a honeycomb beeswax candle. At Christmas time you could fit a pair of pedestal candlesticks with, respectively, a red and green candle and a clutch of seasonal holly, ivy and small spray carnations. So that the design is not top heavy, some flowers and foliage should cascade well below the foam holder and cover at least one-third of the candlestick.

Making your own candles can bring another dimension to table decoration and enable you to colour-match any size and shape of candle you wish to complement any component of your table setting. You can buy candle moulds in a range of shapes – from fir cones and pieces of fruit to cartoon characters and classic sculptures – or you can improvise by using

BELOW: A rainbow-coloured candle, sculptured in the popular American style, has been teamed with individual posies of dried flowers tied with trailing shot-silk ribbons. The table covering is flame-retardant net.

empty egg shells, dessert moulds, yoghurt pots, cardboard tubes and other household items.

Pillar candles, set in tubes, pipes and other cylindrical and rectangular moulds, are especially attractive if they are made in two or more colours – remember to allow each colour to set before you add the next. If the mould is held at an angle before the melted wax is poured in, the diagonal stripes of the finished candle will be more interesting than one composed simply of horizontal stripes.

Plain moulded candles can be embellished in a number of ways to give them more individuality and to make them more striking. You can stick pressed flowers or leaves to the surface of the candle in geometric patterns or in bouquet formations, using a clear paper-craft glue or brushing over the pressed materials with clear, melted wax. You can stick sequins, beads, tiny shells or metal studs – bronze ones are especially effective – in measured rows or in a random pattern, or you can stick on flower, shell and other shapes, cut from gold paper doilies.

If you want a more three-dimensional decoration you can tie ribbon around the base of a pillar candle, finishing it off with either a neat or a full bow. Pleat a length of metal-edged ribbon and wrap it around the candle base, repeating the decoration for napkin rings. You could thread large beads onto leather thong to tie around cylindrical candles, matching the beads colour for colour with the candles and making similar ties for napkin rings to give your table design a lift that takes only moments.

Candles and flowers come together in an unusual way in a design you can see in Chapter 9. Rising majestically from a carpet of colourful blooms, these plain cream altar candles are encircled with a hoop of foliage and blossoms. In a low-key colour grouping, one candle has been ringed with everlasting peas, pansies and marjoram, while another, more extrovert arrangement combines coral-red rowan berries with purple pansies. Dozens of other combinations of colours and textures would look equally effective. This is a useful way of coordinating a table design and an arrangement on a side table or even in an adjacent room. This kind of arrangement requires short-stemmed flowers and leaves only, so off-cuts, snippings and left-overs from larger designs are all that you need.

Some of the items you use to mould poured candles can be retained and used as candle holders in your decoration. Natural items that can be used in this way include oyster and scallop shells, exotic, hollow seedheads, which you can buy from florists' shops, and citrus fruit skins. Household items that can do double-duty as candlewax containers include flowerpots – remember to plug the hole in the base before you pour in the wax – decorative beakers and mugs, preserve jars and brandy glasses. Allow the wax to cool significantly before pouring it into glass containers.

The partnership of candles and water is always a successful one, particularly in summer when you want to create a cool ambience and yet still enjoy the romance of candlelight. You can incorporate one or more candles in a foliage arrangement created to one side of a shallow bowl of water, positioning the candles so that the flames will be prettily reflected in the water. The addition of waterside flowers, such as irises, colour-matched to the candles, adds horticultural variety to a decoration that is equally suitable for a meal indoors or, on a still day, in the garden.

The nightlights and decorative candles that are specially made to float offer another range of design options. (Remember that "ordinary" candles and nightlights will not float; they just topple over.) You can enhance the appearance of plain white nightlights by floating them in a bowl with either pastel or brightly coloured flowers. Lying among, for example, full-blown coral-pink roses or bright yellow pansies, the tiny white candles become nothing more, visually, than flame carriers. Other floating candles are decorative in their own right. Brilliantly coloured star-shaped ones, for example, could be displayed individually, each one in a ramekin dish of water, or as a colourful group in a shallow bowl. Floating candles in more subtle shades and colour combinations of pastel pink with blue, apricot with cream, mint green with mauve and so on will look enchanting if they are allowed to bob about in the water among a scattering of rose or peony petals, a few lawn daisy heads or hydrangea florets. Choose the prettiest bowls or dishes you have for decorations of this kind. Make them as stylish as you can. If you choose a glass bowl, make sure that it is heatproof, for paradoxically, when it is half-filled with water, glass can easily become overheated and crack.

ABOVE: Plain glass tumblers decorated with gold-brushed maple leaves become double images when they stand on a brass plate. The tumblers hold golden, ball-shaped candles, which have their own reflected glory.

BELOW: A cluster of candles in an old blue and white ginger jar and a pair of carved wooden ducks share the spotlight in this impromptu table setting.

TABLE FLOWERS

There are occasions when a scattering of petals or flower heads on the surface of the table is decoration enough. Indeed, there may be times when this casual approach will reinforce the appeal of a table decoration. This is a custom in some north African countries, especially Tunisia, where fresh flowers such as zinnias and godetias will fill almost every space between the plates and the dishes. Delightful as it is to welcome visitors in this way, it may seem wasteful to emulate the custom with fresh flowers, but colourful and fragrant petals from a damask rose or a clove-scented carnation, mixed with fallen leaves or the variegated and aromatic leaves of some varieties of scented geranium or with dried flowers, will look equally attractive. The ones best suited to scattering in this way are strawflowers, which you can buy in some florists' shops. Their fully rounded, daisy-shaped heads look so pretty they might have been grown specially for this purpose.

Foliage and flowers that are growing in pots and bowls make interesting table decorations that can be as stylish as they are varied. You might like to display a bonsai tree, a living sculpture, growing in a shallow black or earth-brown dish; a miniature garden created in the minimalist and restrained Japanese style or, as children like to do, with a more romantic "silver bells and cockle shells" approach. A selection of herbs in pots is appropriate for a summer meal in the garden or the kitchen, and this has the advantage of contributing a medley of fragrances. A cluster of earthenware pots containing basil, thyme, mint, savory and coriander will provide delightfully aromatic, but not overpowering, overtones to a meal that should, if possible, feature at least some of the same herbs in the menu.

If natural earthenware pots do not fit into your scheme of things, you can grow herbs for display in decorative beakers and mugs, in an attractive trough or plastic-lined basket or in a small terrarium. Flowerpots can be disguised in elegant *cache-pots* or other attractive containers, or you can paint them in one or more colours to complement your table arrangement, decorating them with a twist of paper ribbon and large bow.

You will find that paper ribbon has several uses in table decoration. You can use it to tie around candles and table napkins, confident that the bows formed from the stiff material will stay neat and full, just as you made them. You can use it to tie place settings of cutlery, one for each person at a buffet party, and to tie around the stems of drinking glasses to add colour and style. It can be used, too, to wrap around gifts, thoughtful little surprise packages to put by each place at the table. Criss-cross the ribbon each way across a small parcel so that it is perfectly colour-matched to other decorations on the table.

The ribbon is sold in two styles. It can be tightly coiled, when it takes a little time and trouble to unfurl it, or it is sometimes multi-folded in a thin strip. It is available in a wide range of colours, some streaked with gold or silver, and also printed in floral patterns. If you buy a plain ribbon and feel that its matt surface lacks lustre, spatter-spray it with metallic paint so that it sparkles in the light.

Paper and card in other forms can be used to create interesting table decorations – not just place cards and menu cards, but also party crackers, miniature carrier bags to hold flower holders or little gifts, and even place mats and table coverings.

BELOW: A deep, cone-shaped shell is fitted with soaked foam and a deep blue candle, set in a plastic spike. Fern leaves cut from a houseplant have been used to outline the height and width of the decoration, and five yellow lilies reflect the colours of the tableware.

We have already seen how effective gift-wrapping paper and wallpaper can be when they are used instead of tablecloths. You can also cut place mats or cover existing mats with these materials or with coloured card. The shape of a cat's face cut from shiny black card needs no more than a pair of slanting eyes and whiskers of cotton thread to make place mats for a Hallowe'en supper, and balloon shapes can be cut from differently coloured card for a children's party. Our choice in Chapter 5 is for golden apple place mats, with place cards to match.

Small carrier bags, which are simple to fold from a rectangular piece of textured paper or from thin card, can be used to display dried or fresh flowers (when you will need to conceal a small waterproof spice jar to keep them fresh), to hold a selection of after-dinner candies or small toys for children. Tiny paper bags filled with similar items can be hung on table-top trees formed from evergreen branches or bunches of twigs. Make one for each guest, and dismantle the tree ornaments in a goodwill gesture at the end of the party.

RIGHT: A trio of old lustre jugs filled with feverfew leaves and double white spray chrysanthemums strikes a note of informality that is in keeping with the heavily textured table covering, a pastel-coloured Indian rug.

RIGHT: When it's lunch time and you make a spur-of-the-moment decision to eat outside, the table decoration can be impromptu, too. A tall earthenware pot and a few gnarled apple-tree twigs can be swiftly brought into the scheme of things with a trio of bright orange lilies secured with a few twists of fine silver wire.

WORKING TO SCALE

Whether you are gathering a cluster of gnarled and knobbly apple twigs to make a designer tree, creating a party decoration from a preformed cone shape and sugared almonds or composing an exuberant floral centrepiece, it is important to keep the table-top designs in scale. Paintings and etchings from the 18th and 19th centuries show us that big was beautiful in those days. What these illustrations do not convey is the frustration that must have been experienced by the guests who could not talk to their companions on the opposite side of the table, because they could not see through the mesh of flowers and foliage.

In general, it is best to create designs that will be no higher than eye level when your guests are seated. An exception may be pedestal arrangements and those that are composed around the top of footed candlesticks. In these cases, guests may be able to see each other beneath the level of the flowers, and so the social niceties may be preserved.

The matter of scale does not relate to height alone. It is important that you create both floral arrangements and other types of decoration that are in proportion to the size of the table. A centrepiece that is too large – usually larger than a single place setting – could appear to dominate the occasion and divert attention from the food you are serving. On the other hand, a decoration that is too small – a posy of flowers in the centre of a long refectory table, for example – might look meagre and insignificant.

If flowers are in short supply and you have a large, round or long, narrow table, overcome the shortfall by incorporating flowers and foliage in a wider collection of utensils. You could, for example, arrange a cluster of pottery or copper jelly moulds with bright nasturtiums or marigolds arranged in one or two of them, or make the most of your flower stock by displaying each bloom in a specimen flower vase. If you can enlarge the group with a cluster of candles in glass holders the display will look positively generous.

GARLANDS AND SWAGS

Garlands draped around and across tables have a history and symbolism similar to that of wreaths. In ancient times floral garlands were hung around the most important pieces of furniture – especially the banqueting table – as a welcome to honoured guests, but they were also draped around urns, vases and wine jars, too, as a gesture of hospitality.

They are an ideal way of decorating tables not only on highdays and holidays, at weddings and baptisms, Thanksgiving Day and at Christmas, but on other occasions, too. You can simply pin foliage-laden stems of ivy or pastel green hops around the rim of the table or drape them in gentle arcs across the fall of the tablecloth. You can add colour and texture to these supple stems by wiring or gluing on flowers; white spray chrysanthemums look especially pretty nestling among drapes of ivy leaves.

Alternatively, use a core material in place of natural stems and decorate it with flowers and foliage of all kinds. Choose a core material that is in scale with the plant materials you want to use. Coiled paper ribbon is strong enough to support the weight of dried flowers and small-scale fresh ones, but would show signs of strain if, for example, heavy cones or apples formed part of the design. If you choose a paper core that matches the colour of the flowers, the problem of show-through will not occur, because if strips of the paper are revealed as flower posies twist and twirl, it will just seem part of the design.

Other possible materials for a core, in ascending order of size and strength, are string, cord and rope, and wire of various thicknesses. If you decide to create a garland around a length of wire, test it first to check that it will fall into natural-looking curves.

Dried flower garlands of, say, strawflowers and statice, sea lavender and pearl everlasting can be made well in advance of the occasion and, indeed, can be used again and again. Garlands of fresh flowers, which will not have a moisture source, can be partly composed in advance for assembly at the last possible minute. Make up small posies of a single flower type or mixed nosegays of many colours, bind the stems with twine or silver wire and leave the flowers standing in water. It is a simple matter to bind them to the core or, as some florists do, stick the stems to the cord using a hot-glue gun just before your guests arrive.

Whether it is a garland of ivy leaves and wild roses trimming the drinks table for a summer garden party, a drape of petally roses and carnations across the front of the table at a wedding, an edging of evergreens and cones to highlight the Christmas dinner table, or a ribbon of hops trailing among the dishes and plates in an elegantly casual curve, all kinds of garlands and floral ribbons have the potential to lift your table decoration to a new stylistic level.

RIGHT: A floral swag both flatters a table and sets the scene for a memorable occasion. This one is made up of asparagus fern, variegated mint and hollyhock flowers.

Within the space of a single day you might set a breakfast tray with embossed white china, a scarlet table napkin and, linking the two colours, a red and white tray cloth, and the effect would be vibrant and dramatic – a brilliant awakening. At lunchtime you might spread a terracotta-coloured cloth over the table, set out the same tableware, arrange a handful of rust-coloured zinnias in an earthenware pot and tuck deep cream napkins into polished wooden rings. With guests expected in the evening, the tableware might put in its third appearance of the day, but this time on a white textured cloth set with pale pink underplates, sugared-almond pink napkins and soft pink peonies, to create a symphony of white and pastels that is both relaxing and formal.

3 Making Colour Work

UNDERSTANDING COLOUR

In order to make colour work for you, it is helpful to understand why colour harmonies and juxtapositions work in the way they do, in everything from fine art to high fashion, from flower arrangements to table settings. We often use the expression "all the colours of the rainbow" without perhaps realizing how those colours appear and in what order, and without appreciating that the sequence of the colours of the rainbow is the key to the practical and artistic use of colour. A few simple experiments will soon prove the point for you.

Place, for example, a hand-painted ironstone plate, decorated with an oriental design in deep, deep crimson and midnight blue, on a purple place mat – in terms of colour the two items will seem to have been made for each other, and the purple table covering will look as harmonious as could be. For a complete contrast, place the same plate on a yellow tablecloth – the effect will be discordant, for the cloth would look too bright, and the plate would seem less attractive than before.

Another experiment to show how colours are influenced by their surroundings is to place a dark, forest green plate on a bright red place mat or to fill a dark green jug with a branch of brilliant coral-red rowan berries. Each colour, the green and the red, will complement the other and appear all the more vibrant because of their proximity. To achieve a quite different effect, stand the same green plate on a dark blue tray or a mustard-yellow underplate – in both cases the intensity of the green will seem greatly diminished.

To help you understand the reasons for these contrasting effects study the colour wheel on the facing page, which places colours in rainbow order. Many artists seem to know this wheel instinctively. One of the simplest ways of interpreting all the combinations of the formula is to draw a circle, as we have done, and divide it into six equal segments, like the slices of a cake. The three primary colours – red, blue and yellow – are filled in in three alternate segments. In the three blank spaces, are the secondary colours, each of which is achieved by mixing two of the primary colours – that gives you mauve between red and blue, green between blue and yellow, and orange in the last space, the result of mixing yellow and red.

EVEN IF YOU HAVE only a single set of tableware, you can create a table setting to suit the time of day, the occasion and the mood of the moment with simple alterations to the tablecloth and accessories. White, which is by far the most popular choice for dinner services, does not restrict you to a wall-to-wall white table setting or, no matter what its shape and style, to table schemes that are inescapably either wholly formal or wholly informal.

More than anything, it is the way you use colour in the table covering, the accessories and the decorations that characterizes the setting. A table that is set with chestnut-brown china can look as sophisticated as one set with white, while a dinner service with delicate bands of gold leaf can look fabulous on a gold and green tapestry cloth and just as stunning on a multi-patterned table covering of gift wrapping paper.

ABOVE: The wide gold bands, highlighting the depth of the flatware and accenting the hollow-ware, are echoed in the broad stripes of the blue and white table covering. Napkins in crisp white would be a perfect choice.

THE COLOUR WHEEL

To make colour work the way you want it to in your table decorations it is a good idea to make a quick "ready reckoner" of the colour spectrum, known as a colour wheel. Draw a rough circle, divide it into six segments and colour or write the names of the three primary colours – red, yellow and blue – in alternate spaces. Colour the three secondary colours in the blank segments, orange – a mixture of red and yellow – between those colours, then green, and lastly violet. Then you have only to glance at the wheel to see which colour partnerships or trios will give you the boldest or most subdued effects.

A ring of lime-green lady's mantle and cornflowers, for example, would be an unusual but reasonably restrained floral combination for a midsummer party decoration, because green and blue are neighbours on the colour wheel. But add a dash of red – which is opposite green and next-but-one to blue on the wheel – and you have a stunning colour blend. Add the red ingredient in the form of luscious strawberries, and your guests will be drooling!

The combination of red and blue, both strong primary colours when they are used at full strength – in deep shades – can be striking, even elegant, but for a much softer and younger looking expression of these colours, select flowers in pastel tints of pink and palest blue.

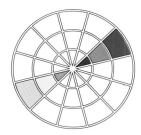

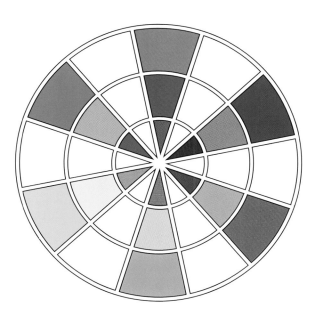

Wheel 2: *Complementary colours*

Wheel 1: *Primary and secondary colours; Tints and Tones*

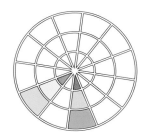

Wheel 3: *Harmonious colours*

Those six segments give you the basic hues, but not all green tableware is mid-green nor is every yellow table napkin mid-yellow. Therefore, to make the wheel more helpful still it is best to shade in the varying gradations of each hue. You can make tints by mixing each hue with different proportions of white, and tones by mixing each one with different amounts of black. Thus the blue segment on the colour wheel, for example, could be graded from a nearly white pastel tint with only a hint of blue, through mid-blue, the pure colour, to deep, dark, nearly black, navy blue mixed with the greatest proportion of black.

In artists' terms, colours that face or oppose each other on the wheel are said to be complementary. That is why green tableware displayed on red place mats will look vibrant and bright. It is the reason, too, that several of the designs in Chapter 4, which were composed almost by instinct, feature red in some way – in the table coverings, the fruit, flowers, napkin rings and candles. Naturally, not all the greens are pure and not all the reds are bright scarlet. It is the mixing and blending of tints and shades that make the use of colour so interesting and challenging.

You may have a set of deep sage green plates or dessert bowls, which is not, perhaps, the most

scintillating of colours, or a green tablecloth that, because of the proportion of black used in the dye, is going on grey. Those are just the situations that call for a hint, or more than that, of red to intensify the green. You could make a table wreath of rosy red apples and deep green leaves, tie a hand-arranged posy of fallen red leaves, crimson hydrangeas and green seedheads with a shimmering ribbon, or provide accents of colour with napkin rings bound with vivid coral-red berries.

Colours that are next to each other on the colour wheel are known as harmonious shades. This term is appropriate because, in any of the three possible pairings, one of the adjacent colours will be a primary – red, blue or yellow – and the other a secondary colour, in part derived from it.

To continue with our example using green tableware, it is possible to create an harmonious scheme by moving in two opposite directions. If you team green-rimmed plates with dark blue place mats and table napkins, you will create a cool, almost moody setting. Move the other way around the wheel, to primary yellow, and you can set green-patterned plates on a yellow cloth, decorate the table with lemon-coloured lilies and golden freesias so that it looks as if the sun is streaming in, even on the dullest of days.

USING THREE COLOURS

You can extend the look of artistic harmony by adding another colour, one that is on one or other side of the two adjacent hues. If you add purple and other shades of mauve to an intrinsically blue and green setting – decorating the table with a bowl of pansies or placing a posy of mint, chive and marjoram flowers on each plate – you simply extend the harmonious effect. None of the colours, regardless of its tint or tone, will be predominant. On the other hand, if you were to add orange marigolds and lilies to the basic blue and green setting, they would dominate the colour scheme.

In the same way, the oriental red and blue plate mentioned earlier would be in complete harmony with a purple table covering or decoration but would be in danger of being overshadowed by a yellow one.

There might be occasions when you want to go for a bold effect in your table setting and create a scheme that is uncompromisingly and uninhibitedly over the top in terms of colour. You can do this by teaming all three primary colours or all three secondary colours – mauve, green and orange – in what is known as a triadic scheme. Just how uninhibited such a scheme would appear depends on the tints and shades of the colours you use. Spatter-painted plates in pale tones of red, blue and yellow are illustrated in Chapter 9, where they have been placed on a strongly patterned table covering in deeper shades of those colours – peony red, dense blue and golden yellow. The setting is bright and arresting, but would be far more so if the tableware were decorated with solid blocks of colour.

Taking a completely different approach to the use of colour on the table, it can be immensely effective to use a single colour and team it with either white or black. Both of these are considered to be neutral and therefore, in colour terms, not to count.

RIGHT: When the mood is casual and the tableware French provincial style, a hand-arranged posy of wild flowers, seedheads and russet hydrangea heads looks fresher than a vertical decoration. A few red-going-on-gold leaves have been included for their brilliant colour, and the bunch is tied with gilt-edged ribbon.

ACHIEVING EFFECTS WITH MONOCHROMES

Artists and decorators from the East well understand how effective the restrained or minimal use of colour can be. The Japanese-inspired setting in Chapter 7 is all the more striking because, with the tableware and table covering in sparkling white, the only "real" colour (unless you count the prawns) is found in the brown wooden rice steamers, the contorted twig and – still in the brown-going-on-yellow segment of the wheel – the yellow quince.

Also in Chapter 7 are two western interpretations of this monochromatic concept. In one, white embossed plates are shown with an embroidered white cotton napkin, a white orchid and – in a truly minimalist use of colour – a twist of green iris leaves as a napkin tie. The other contrasts the whiter-than-white tableware with a lighter, duller green in the form of a bay leaf decoration, tissue paper present wrappings and a ribbon ring around the crisp, white cotton napkin. The full-blown, just off-white rose adds a hint of warm tints, and the gold highlights on the sage green decorations preclude the tendency that this colour has towards excessive light absorption.

Just as it can be extremely effective to arrange a table in a variety of tints and shades of a single colour, so it can be both stylish and rewarding to treat white as a basic colour and team it with pastel tints, ranging from buttermilk through to deep, rich cream. There are, however, certain pitfalls to such a scheme, and it is best to bear them in mind before you reach the bewildering and disconcerting stage of knowing that something has not gone quite according to plan.

If, for example, your plates and dishes are pure white and you want to introduce the softening effect of warm cream tints, be sure to do so in such a way that the scheme looks as if you meant it and not as if the various items are, in colour terms, an accidental near-miss. This can happen when, for example, you use a damask tablecloth and table napkins that are only just off-white. When you place sparkling white tableware on it, the linen could look faded and jaded rather than mellow. To avoid this situation, it is better to use a slightly intensified tint of cream so that the difference is more marked. You could also arrange a bowl of white and cream roses and introduce a second colour in both the floral decoration and the napkin ties.

In a similar way, if you have cream tableware, and especially if it is antique, it can be a mistake to display it with uncompromisingly white table linen. For an arrangement in Chapter 4, for which we photographed a set of delightful pottery plates with a green and red border decoration, we chose deep cream embroidered napkins, which tone perfectly with the tableware and avoid any hint that it is in any way discoloured.

Sometimes, if you are planning, say, a white on white or a green on green table setting with one predominant colour, there can be a problem of definition. If there is a perfect colour match between the tableware and the tablecloth, the plates can be almost lost to the eye, especially if the cloth has little or no distinguishing texture. One way to overcome this is to introduce underplates in a contrasting colour. These plates, which are slightly larger than dinner plates and which remain on the table throughout the meal, provide continuity of colour.

You will see several examples of this decorative ploy throughout the book. In some cases the underplates have been used to help the colour definition; in others they provide textural contrast; and in others, when brass or glass plates are used, they add sparkle and highlights. Shell-edged plates have been placed over brown and cream striped ones, and those same striped plates were placed over embossed white underplates with the contrasting feature of a scalloped edge. Glass plates are used over stylish brown and white china and, in an arrangement that is vaguely medieval, over scrubbed wooden bread boards. In a scheme like this, illustrated in Chapter 6, table settings have come full circle since the times when food was served first on slices of bread and later on wooden trenchers.

RIGHT: Deep cream plates, decorated with a hand-painted leaf and fruit motif, have been set on a cream muslin cloth. The cream, lace-edged napkins have been tied with red cord, and the creamware jugs have been filled with evergreens and cranberries. Red and green honeycomb beeswax candles, tied into bundles, can be placed in shallow bowls or ramekin dishes and lighted as they are to make a colourful quartet.

LEFT: In an association of ideas, gold-sprayed cardboard leaves have been arranged as an "underplate" around each setting of plates with their double bands of gold, and the theme is taken up by the napkin circlet.

PART  TWO

You might have dark green plates that are as densely coloured as any holly leaves; your tableware may be decorated with broad leaf-green bands; or your creamware plates may be ringed around with a design of evergreen leaves and berries. You may have a set of avocado green baking dishes and serving bowls, or some heavy pottery plates, decorated with an embossed pattern of gourds and trailing vines. You may have a green marbled teaset, a reminder of the leisurely Victorian era, or chunky pottery soup bowls that look as if they have been spattered with leaf-green raindrops.

If green is your colour, the decorations in this section will show you how you can enhance your tableware still further by teaming it with natural decorations. Choose from a hand-arranged posy of lettuce leaves or a made-in-moments plate posy of fallen leaves and marigold petals. Make a celebratory wreath of polished apples or an exuberant display of lilies and freesias, arranged in a melon shell. Tie green-edged table napkins with a twist of chive leaves, and hold embroidered lace napkins together with a printed paper band.

4 Go for Green!

RIGHT: A heavy woven tablecloth provides an ideal setting for an informal lunch or supper.

The Leafy Look

This hand-arranged posy of lettuce leaves and garden flowers takes its cue from the green and white cabbage-leaf plates and soup tureen. The decoration is placed in a shallow bowl of water on one of the dinner plates.

YOU WILL NEED

selection of flowers, such as
    roses, marigolds, everlasting
    pea, nasturtium, verbena and
    clary
12–14 outer lettuce leaves
fine silver wire
florist's scissors

1 Hold one of the largest flowers, in this case a rose, in one hand and arrange four lettuce leaves around it. Continue to hold the group at the base as you add leaves and flowers.

2 Arrange more flowers, such as verbena and everlasting pea, around the outside of the leaves, then add another ring of lettuce leaves. You may like to bind the stems with silver wire to secure them at this stage.

3 Continue adding flowers and leaves, then bind the stems close to the base. Push in more flowers so that the colour is distributed evenly.

Berry Bright

Clusters of bright rowan berries and glossy evergreen fronds
are bound to make an impact in this country-style napkin ring.

YOU WILL NEED

fine silver wire
rowan berries
short sprays of evergreens
florist's scissors
medium-gauge wire
wire cutters

1 Twist the wire to form a
ring, overlapping the ends and
twisting them tightly together.
Bind small sprays of berries and
evergreens to the ring with
silver wire, positioning them so
that the stems of one spray are
covered by the tips of the next.
Continue all around the ring
until it is covered.

2 Fold a napkin in half and in
half again, and then fold under
the two sides, to leave a
triangle. Ease the point through
the berry ring.

RIGHT: A checked, multi-
coloured table napkin unifies
the reds and the green, and is a
less predictable choice than a
plain one.

RIGHT: You could decorate the ring with red or green candles but a trio of different colours is more unusual. Small, firm pears or satsumas could be used to create a fruit ring in a similar way.

Apple Harvest

Whether you are planning a harvest supper, a Hallowe'en party in a barn or a Christmas buffet, this ring of rosy apples will strike a festive note.

YOU WILL NEED

small red apples
medium-gauge stub wires
preformed dry foam ring, 25cm/
    10in in diameter
3 plastic candle spikes
    (available from florists' shops)
apple leaves or evergreen leaves,
    such as ivy
3 candles, 2.5cm/1in in diameter

1 Wire each apple. Push a stub wire through it, cross over the two ends close to the fruit and twist them together. To give the decoration variety, wire some of the apples at the base, some at one side and some at the top.

2 Begin to arrange the apples close together around the ring so that they cover the top and both sides. Position the three candle spikes between the apples.

3 Fill in the ring with leaves facing this way and that until all the foam is covered. Insert the candles in the plastic holders and check that the bases are hidden by leaves.

ABOVE: Welcome each guest with a colourful and sweet-smelling herb posy and place a small glass of water beside each setting to keep the leaves fresh through the meal. Mint and marjoram, purple sage and pansies, clary and chives have lengths of raffia tied around their short-cut stems. Heavily-textured jade place mats are set over a purple and green striped cloth.

ABOVE: Soup dishes with hand-painted rims are perfectly complemented by a vegetable soup garnished with blobs of crème fraîche and chive leaves tied into knots. More herb leaves encircle the green and white napkins and are tied around the stems of golden-yellow spray chrysanthemums. Complete with green-rimmed Mexican wine glasses, the setting would be appropriate for an alfresco lunch.

LEFT: High on style and low on housework, these jade green paper plates and broad-striped gift-wrap are an ideal choice for a children's party. The fierce-looking dragons can be take-home souvenirs.

LEFT: Evoke a more leisurely era by setting a celebration tea table with mottled green china, a gilded china teapot and pansies. The cutlery has been tied with shot-silk ribbons in mauve, blue and green.

BELOW LEFT: Patterned plates can provide a variety of leads for table decoration of all kinds, and this one is no exception. A plate painted from side to side with holly leaves and berries prompts a profusion of berries spilling out of a rectangular vase, and a knife rest, which repeats the painted motif, is formed from a holly twig entwined with ribbon.

BELOW: Set green porcelain tableware on a velvety red cloth and you have two complementary colours – ones that are opposite on the colour wheel – each bringing out the best in the other. If you display each place setting with a twist of striped ribbon you will build an effective colour bridge between the two.

Plate Posy

Fallen leaves and leaves snipped from houseplants have been arranged in concentric circles on a dinner plate to create an unusual and two-dimensional centrepiece.

YOU WILL NEED

selection of leaves in varying
    colours, shapes and sizes,
    such as maple, periwinkle and
    scented geranium
marigolds
dinner plate

1 Wipe the fallen leaves with a damp cloth to remove any dirt and polish glossy leaves with a dry cloth. Arrange the largest leaves in an overlapping ring around the outside of the plate. Arrange subsequent rows to contrast in shape and colour. Place a marigold in the centre and scatter petals over the leaves.

RIGHT: Solve the knotty problem of how to present table napkins by tying them in knots. To do this, open out the napkin, wrong side upwards, and fold the two side points to the centre. Fold the two sides in again to make a long strip, and tie a loose knot in the centre. Push a few flowers into the knot.

Pot Luck

Mix and match the seasons by arranging spring-time yellow flowers in a hollowed-out melon shell. A heap of gourds, and plates depicting other squashes, complete the autumnal theme.

YOU WILL NEED

melon
knife
tablespoon
block of absorbent stem-holding
  foam, soaked in water
light, variegated foliage, such as
  pineapple mint
selection of flowers, such as
  lilies and freesias
florist's scissors

1 Cut a slice from the top of the melon. Use the tablespoon to scoop out the melon seeds and flesh, and reserve them. Take care that you do not pierce the fruit skin. Cut a thin sliver from the base of the melon shell so that it will stand steady. Trim the block of foam and place it in the shell, then arrange the foliage sprays to give the design height and width.

2 Position the lilies so that they follow the outlines set by the stems of the foliage. Because this is an "all-round" design, make sure that it is equally attractive from all sides.

3 Arrange the freesias between the lilies where their sharper colour will form an attractive contrast.

LEFT: If your dining table is a long, narrow one, you could position the melon decoration in the centre and arrange a bowl of gourds on either side to bring the whole composition closer to the guests at each end. (Green and cream pottery from Evans Kitchen Shop)

Spice Basket

Decorative baskets with built-in aroma can be clustered in the centre of the table or placed close to each place setting. These "log cabin" baskets are made of cinnamon sticks glued to plastic flowerpots.

YOU WILL NEED

cinnamon sticks
hot glue gun or clear, quick-setting glue
rectangular flowerpots with sloping sides
ribbon for handles (we used plaited banana leaves)
rowan berries, cranberries, nuts, gold and silver coloured candies or dried spices to fill the baskets

1 Measure the cinnamon sticks to size and stick them to all four sides of the flowerpots. You will be able to compensate for the sloping sides by positioning the thick end of the spice sticks at the top of the holders.

2 Glue more cinnamon sticks horizontally at the top and bottom of the baskets. Stick a length of ribbon inside each basket, attaching the ends to opposite sides.

LEFT: Japanese rice bowls in rich sage green are colour-matched to the banana leaf ribbon handles. These decorations could be filled with candies and offered as take-home gifts or hung from bare twigs or fir branches as an arrangement for a side table. (Ribbon by V. V. Rouleaux)

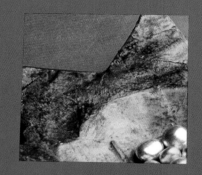

There is more than a hint of luxury about tableware that is decorated with fine gold leaf. The ornamentation may be no more than a narrow rim around the edge of each plate, or it might be as richly ornamental as an embossed pattern of a flight of angels picked out in gold, or it could be as discreet as a ring of, symbolically, gold leaves around each piece of flatware and hollow-ware. If your principal set of tableware is in this style, it can be stimulating to think about the other ways you can present it – on anything from a paisley-pattern wool cloth to a richly embroidered tapestry, from starched white cotton to printed gift-wrapping paper, with decorations as diverse as gold-painted eggs and gold-stencilled table napkins.

If you do not have any gold-patterned china, you can still enter the table setting gold rush with plates that are as bold as brass or as impertinent as paper. Inexpensive, fun and disposable, gold paper plates enable you to put on the style and pile on the simulation with no hint of ostentation.

5 Glorious Gold

RIGHT: These crackers are sure to make the party go off with a bang! Two of them are made in gold-marbled wrapping paper to tone with the paisley wool tablecloth, and another is a glitzy all-gold.

Plain Crackers

Make your own party crackers for Christmas or for another celebration, and you can colour-match them to your table scheme. Marbled gift-wrapping and foil-backed papers can be used to make some of the smartest decorations in town.

YOU WILL NEED

For each cracker
cardboard roll 4.5cm/1¾in in
    diameter, 22.5cm/8¾in long
    (such as the inner roll from
    kitchen or lavatory paper)
craft knife
decorative paper, 18.5 × 33cm/
    7¼ × 13¼in
1 or more trinkets and toys
1 cardboard "bang" strip
    (available from joke shops
    and novelty shops)
ruler
pencil
double-sided adhesive tape
fine silver wire
trimmings, such as gold beads
    and braid
hot glue gun or clear, quick-
    setting glue

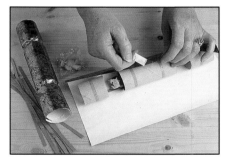

1 Cut the cardboard roll in half and cut one section in half again. Place the decorative paper face down and position the longest piece of cardboard tube in the centre of one long edge. Position the other two rolls 4cm/1½in to either side of it. Insert the trinket or toy in the centre roll and push the snap through all three. Secure the cardboard tubes to the edge of the paper with the adhesive tape.

2 Press three strips of adhesive tape to the opposite edge of the paper. Tightly roll up the paper to enclose the cardboard tubes and press the roll onto the adhesive strips.

3 Pinch the two "waists" between the cardboard rolls. Cut short lengths of silver wire and bind the gathered-up paper tightly.

4 Trim the crackers in any way you like – by sticking gold braid around the edges, by gluing gold beading round the centre or by wrapping bands and tying bows of gold-thread ribbons.

Complete Elevation

Pedestal candlesticks can be readily adapted to become high-rise flower containers. This one, which began as a bargain from a charity shop, has been given a face-lift that makes it look like verdigris.

YOU WILL NEED

inexpensive glass, china or
    wooden candlestick
acrylic paints in gold, green and
    bronze
small, fine paintbrushes
plastic candle-cup saucer, from
    florists
florist's adhesive clay
cylinder of absorbent stem-
    holding foam, soaked in water
florist's adhesive tape
selection of plant materials, such
    as hops, fennel flowerheads,
    variegated pineapple mint,
    spray chrysanthemums, white
    marguerites, scented
    geranium leaves
florist's scissors

1 Dab spots of gold acrylic paint all over the surface of the candlestick.

2 Before the gold paint dries, dab all over the surface with green paint and then with the bronze to fill in all the spaces. Leave the candlestick to dry.

3 To adapt the candlestick to a flower container, cut strips of adhesive clay and stick them to the underside of the plastic saucer. Press this firmly to the candlestick and insert the soaked foam. Hold it in place with criss-cross lines of adhesive tape, taken from side to side of the plastic holder.

4 Arrange a cascade of hops to trail over the rim of the plastic holder and almost half-way down the candlestick. Arrange the fennel to give height and width to the arrangement, keeping it in roughly a ball shape. Arrange first the spray chrysanthemums and then the marguerites. Fill in with pineapple mint and geranium leaves.

LEFT: The green and gold of the floral arrangement is repeated through the candles and napkins to complete the setting.

Project Outline

Plain table napkins can be given a spark of individuality when they are stencilled with gold fabric paint. You could decorate plain place mats or the corners of a tablecloth in a similar way.

YOU WILL NEED

plain cotton napkin
pineapple stencil (available from
    craft shops)
gold fabric paint
small, fine paintbrush

1 Position the stencil carefully in the centre of one corner of the napkin. Hold it firmly in place with one hand and dab on the paint from directly above. Take care that the brush hairs do not cause the paint to run under the stencil. Decorate another corner of the napkin in the same way. Leave the paint to dry thoroughly. Follow the washing instructions carefully when the napkin is laundered.

LEFT: Blue-handled cutlery coordinates with the colour of the napkin, and the gold candle echoes the shape of the pineapple motif. The table covering, a simulated cloth of gold, is textured, high-gloss paper.

BELOW: It might be a New Year's Eve party, a golden wedding celebration, or just for fun – whatever the occasion, this is the way to keep the style up and the costs down. Gold paper plates have been partnered with black paper serviettes, folded into cone shapes and decorated with bow ties of coloured card. The "money" and the candies are spilling out of used food cans, sprayed gold and covered with gold sequin trim.

ABOVE: A remnant of furnishing fabric printed with sun, moon and star images has been used as a tablecloth in this galactic setting. The golden table napkins, folded into quarters, are pushed into inexpensive brass rings decorated with sun and moon shapes, and the cutlery has been tied in golden cord.

LEFT: White china with a gold fern-leaf pattern is a dramatic contrast with the black cotton table napkins trimmed with gold braid and tassels. Flashes of colour in the present trimmings and the party cracker emphasize the starkness of the main scheme.

ABOVE: Gold-coloured papier mâché dishes bring out the golden highlights in the tissue-paper-edged plate and napkin rings. When you mix and match plain and fancy tableware like this, each item seems to bring out the best properties of the others.

RIGHT: Are the trails of ivy natural? Is it a "real" ribbon bow? Or have they all been lifted from the gift-wrap table covering? The idea for the ivy stems and the golden thread bow *was* lifted from the paper design, so no wonder they are a perfect match. Individual table presents wrapped in the same paper pay lip service to the paper's intended purpose.

RIGHT: To decorate the napkin, make a loop with the gossamer ribbon and sew the two ends. Tie more ribbon in a bow, trim the ends slantwise and tack it to the napkin-ring loop. Slip the ribbon loop and the loop on the angel tree decoration on one corner of the napkin and fold over the corner. Scatter other golden angels over the tablecloth.

Renaissance Style

This table setting is pure Renaissance – red-dyed eggs decorated with silver and gold, napkins tied with gossamer ribbon bows and embellished with golden angels, and a sumptuous cloth of red and gold.

YOU WILL NEED

red edible food colouring
eggs
non-toxic gold and silver felt-
    tipped pens
non-toxic gold spray paint
    (optional)

1 Bring some water to the boil in a small pan and add a few drops of food colouring until you achieve the depth of colour you like. Hard-boil the eggs in the coloured water and leave them to cool and dry. Draw swirls, curls and dotted lines on the eggs with the gold and silver pens to create elaborate patterns. If you wish, spray some eggs all over with the gold paint. Leave to dry.

Roll Up, Roll Up!

Make your own honeycomb beeswax candles and arrange them in your favourite candlesticks or, as here, around a gnarled and twisted vine log. As the candles burn, you will find the gentle aroma of honey absolutely enchanting!

YOU WILL NEED

To make four candles, each 18cm/7in high
sheet of paper for template
metal ruler
craft knife
2 sheets of rolled honeycomb beeswax, 34 × 20cm/ 13½ × 8in
cardboard to protect the working surface
2 lengths of medium-thickness candle wick, each 35cm/14in long

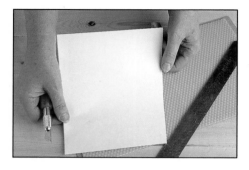

1 Cut the paper to the size of the sheet of beeswax. Measure and mark a point 16cm/6¼in along one long side and a point, measured from the same end, 18cm/7in along the other long side. Draw a line to join the two marks. Cut the paper along this line. Place the beeswax sheet on the cardboard and position the template on one end of the sheet.

2 Using the rule as a guide, cut along the edge of the template. Use long, firm strokes to avoid tearing the beeswax.

3 Cut the wick in half. Place one of the beeswax sheets with the sloping edge on the left and the longer of the two parallel edges towards you. Place the wick close to this longer edge and turn over the edge of the beeswax sheet to enclose it.

4 Tightly roll up the beeswax, taking care to keep the straight edge, which will be at the base of the candle, straight. The other edge, at the top, will have a characteristically graduated line.

RIGHT: Four honeycomb beeswax candles burn brightly around a craggy vine log. Brown and red vine leaves are trailed around the wood, and gilded leaves decorate the table napkin.

Chestnut-brown china with a pattern of twirling leaves and petals; sunflower-yellow representational plates that prompt the dramatic decorative use of one perfect and gigantic flower; mustard-yellow plates, which will allow you to go to town or up-country; sparkling white tableware enlivened with broad yellow bands; or wooden boards used for underplates, as trenchers used to be – tableware in fired-earth colours, woody browns and sunshine yellow, has a whole spectrum of colour potential.

You can team this china with leafy green or sophisticated purple, with toning tan or pearly white. You can create down-to-earth decorations with bunches of carrots and sweetcorn or baskets of autumn vegetables and posies of zingy flowers. You can create a harvest tableau with wheat and field poppies or a penthouse-suite setting with waxy white lilies and mother-of-pearl. You can put a spark into toast-brown table settings by using gold-sprayed cones and gold-painted eggs, shimmering leaf decorations and flickering honeycomb candles. With tableware in the brown-going-on-yellow range, there is every reason to be fired with enthusiasm.

6 Fired-earth Colours

Vegetable Matters

Harness all the bright colours and contrasting shapes of young vegetables to make a spectacular ring for a table centre. The bunches are tied with strands of raffia and wired to a vine wreath form.

YOU WILL NEED

selection of vegetables, such as
   young carrots, green beans,
   spring onions, baby sweet
   corn and chillies
raffia
scissors
medium-gauge stub wires
vine wreath ring, 25cm/10in in
   diameter
herbs, such as pineapple mint

1 Grade the vegetables for size and tie them into small bunches with several strands of raffia.

2 Push a stub wire through the back of the raffia loops, cross over the two ends of the wire and twist them tightly together. To attach the bunches to the ring, push the wires between the interwoven twigs. Arrange the bunches close together, alternating colours and textures to create the most impact, and fill in any gaps with sprigs of herbs. Lightly spray the ring with water and leave it in the refrigerator until just before the meal is ready.

RIGHT: You can make the wheatsheaf from the kind of wheat you can buy in florists' shops. The decoration will look equally effective standing in an earthenware flowerpot as it would hanging on a kitchen wall.

Wheatsheaf

Any meal in a country-style kitchen, from breakfast to supper, will be enhanced by a decoration made from material seemingly gathered from the wayside. The sheaf of wheat and plate posy, both made in moments, perfectly capture that mood.

YOU WILL NEED

bunch of wheat with straight,
    upright heads
florist's scissors
raffia
grasses

1 To make the wheatsheaf, cut the stems of the wheat to even lengths, about 25cm/10in long. Hold a few of the stems in your hand and twist them to the left.

2 Add more stems and twist them in the same direction. Tie the stems tightly with raffia, just below the heads, then loop a bunch of grasses around them. Trim off the stalks at an angle. *Note:* To give wild poppies the longest possible vase life, burn the stem ends over a candle or safety match flame to seal in the sappy substance. Put the flowers in water immediately.

RIGHT: Mustard-yellow china goes ethnic with a cascade of leaves arranged in a hollowed-out seed pod, a scattering of prickly seedheads and a basket of nuts. The printed cotton napkin includes warm red tones, which are repeated in the lychees. The table covering is inexpensive beach matting.

ABOVE: A hoop of spray chrysanthemums and white, daisy-like marguerites is pretty enough for a bridal table. Create romantic napkin rings as miniature versions of a bridal headdress or shower bouquet.

RIGHT: The contrast between terracotta and deep, dark turquoise is a strong and effective one. The mahogany napkin ring has been decorated with a gold-brushed bay leaf and a hydrangea floret, and clusters of the deep red flowers have been used to decorate the paper table covering.

ABOVE: Representational plates can often give a strong lead for decorative notions. These sunflower plates suggest a dramatic display of golden-orange dahlias in an earthenware jug and, just for fun, a giant-sized flower on one of the plates. A trail of willow leaves tucked into the napkin provides the colour contrast.

TOP RIGHT: Mustard-yellow plates can be dressed up for formal occasions or go up-country for a casual meal with family and friends. Here, the table has been set with purple place mats, and each napkin has been slipped into a band made from embroidered braid. A pansy at each place setting provides the perfect finishing touch.

BELOW: Warm terracotta pottery with a strong leaf pattern around the rim is shown with glass fruit plates and cutlery with mother-of-pearl handles. The waxy lilies and embroidered linen napkins complement the striking design of the tableware.

Good Enough to Eat!

A basket of flowers, fruit and vegetables, but with a difference. This is elegant enough to grace the most formal of occasions, but simple enough to compose on the spur of the moment.

YOU WILL NEED

selection of vegetables and fruit, such as garlic, mushrooms, cauliflower, limes and bunches of baby sweetcorn
medium-gauge stub wires
plastic liner
block of absorbent stem-holding foam, soaked in water
rectangular basket
fennel seedheads
lilies

1 Begin by wiring the fruit and vegetables. Push a stub wire through the stalk of each mushroom, cross over the two ends of the wire at the base and twist them together. Wire the garlic heads, cauliflower florets and limes in the same way.

2 Place the plastic liner and soaked foam in the basket. Arrange the vegetables and limes to cover the foam, placing some so that they extend beyond the basket rim.

3 Position some bunches of baby sweetcorn, and arrange the fennel seedheads between the vegetables and limes. Position the lilies at varying heights, with some close to the basket rim and others outlining the full height of the decoration. Fill in any gaps with more fennel. Check that the arrangement is equally pleasing from all sides.

LEFT: Welcome guests at the table with a sweet-smelling posy of fennel seedheads and pineapple mint. The colours of the herbs echo those of the tableware and the painted table and form a bridge between the yellow and the dark green of the napkins. (Tableware: Malvern by Royal Doulton)

RIGHT: With the pressed leaf ring and the brown pottery so closely colour coordinated, there is room for a complete contrast in the table covering and the napkins. A heavily textured deep turquoise cloth and napkins provide just that element of sharpness.

Circlet of Leaves

Gather handfuls of fallen leaves, cut others sparingly from herbs and houseplants and press them in a flower press or between sheets of absorbent paper in heavy books. Dry wing-like seedpods, too, and bring them together in a collage circlet, which can take the place of an underplate.

YOU WILL NEED

cardboard ring, 25cm/10in in
   diameter and 6cm/2½in wide
papercraft glue
pressed leaves, such as birch,
   maple, mint, nettle, sweet
   cicely, lady's mantle and rose
dried winged seed carriers, such
   as lime
gold craft powder
small craft paintbrush

1 Cover the cardboard ring with the least attractive leaves and then, using the glue sparingly, cover them with a patchwork of contrasting leaves until the cardboard is completely covered. Stick the seed carriers over the leaves in a random pattern. Leave the ring to dry.

2 Lightly dust the completed ring with gold craft powder, but do not cover the leaves completely. The powder should provide highlights without disguising the characteristics of the foliage.

ABOVE: The understated decoration of the brown and white plates is continued in the beige napkins, textured paper carrier bags and floral patterned wood blocks. Then the colour takes off – in the woven tablecloth and the brilliant turquoise napkin tie and, for even more contrast, the thick clusters of rowan berries.

LEFT: The least expensive plates and dishes around, moulded as they are from dried banana leaves, and they are cheap enough, but far too stylish, to be disposable. Arrange them with a selection of fruits, nuts, popcorn, potato chips and other snacks for a party (but not with "runny" foods such as soft cheeses), or pile them high for guests to use for sandwiches and other finger foods. When it comes to the table covering, keep it simple – painted wood, scrubbed pine, heavily textured cotton or linen-look paper would all capture the mood.

ABOVE: When flowers are in short supply or if you want to show off a collection of copper moulds, scent bottles or antique jugs, group them centre-stage on the table to supplement or even replace a table decoration. Two small copper jugs filled with herbs and garden flowers draw attention to the firelight gleam of the moulds in a grouping that could be arranged to reflect the shape of a round, square or rectangular table.

ABOVE: The shimmer of pearls is everywhere in this highly individual setting. The brown and white striped plate has been used as an underplate for one transformed with an edging of craggy, glistening shells (instructions for making these are in Chapter 7). The cutlery has mother-of-pearl handles, and the pottery candlesticks and the plastic napkin ring simulate the sheen and the colours without placing too great a strain on the budget.

LEFT: Small, nearly round larch cones are glued together to form a ring around the beeswax candle, and glued to a wire ring to decorate the napkin. A spatter-spray of gold paint catches the flicker of the candlelight and teams with the dried and painted eggshells (instructions for making these are in Chapter 5).

The Wild Side

The combination of wild foods and exotic flowers can be exciting, especially when, at the two extremes, a decoration features dried parasol mushrooms and pastel-coloured lilies. The holder is a twisted willow ring set over the plate.

YOU WILL NEED

3 large dried mushrooms
medium-gauge stub wires
twisted white willow ring,
    25cm/10in in diameter
plate
absorbent stem-holding foam,
    soaked in water
flowers, such as lilies, irises and
    spray chrysanthemums
florist's scissors
dry sphagnum moss

1 Trim the mushroom stalks so that they are graded in height. Push three or four stub wires up through the stalk and bend over the ends, to give a double thickness of the wires to serve as false stalks.

2 Place the willow ring on the plate and fill the centre with pieces of soaked foam. Position the two tallest mushrooms and check that they are secure. If they are not, wrap two wires around the base of the natural stalk and push the ends into the foam. Position the irises and lilies around the base of the decoration.

3 Make a cluster of spray chrysanthemums close to the ring, with other, taller stalks extending almost to the height of the tallest mushroom. Position the third mushroom close to the willow ring and fill in the design with more flowers. Spread the dry moss between the stems.

LEFT: The yellow and blue flowers in the decoration are colour-matched to the table-top and the tableware. A pile of dried sweetcorn extends both the colour and the concept of the edible fungi as a table decoration.

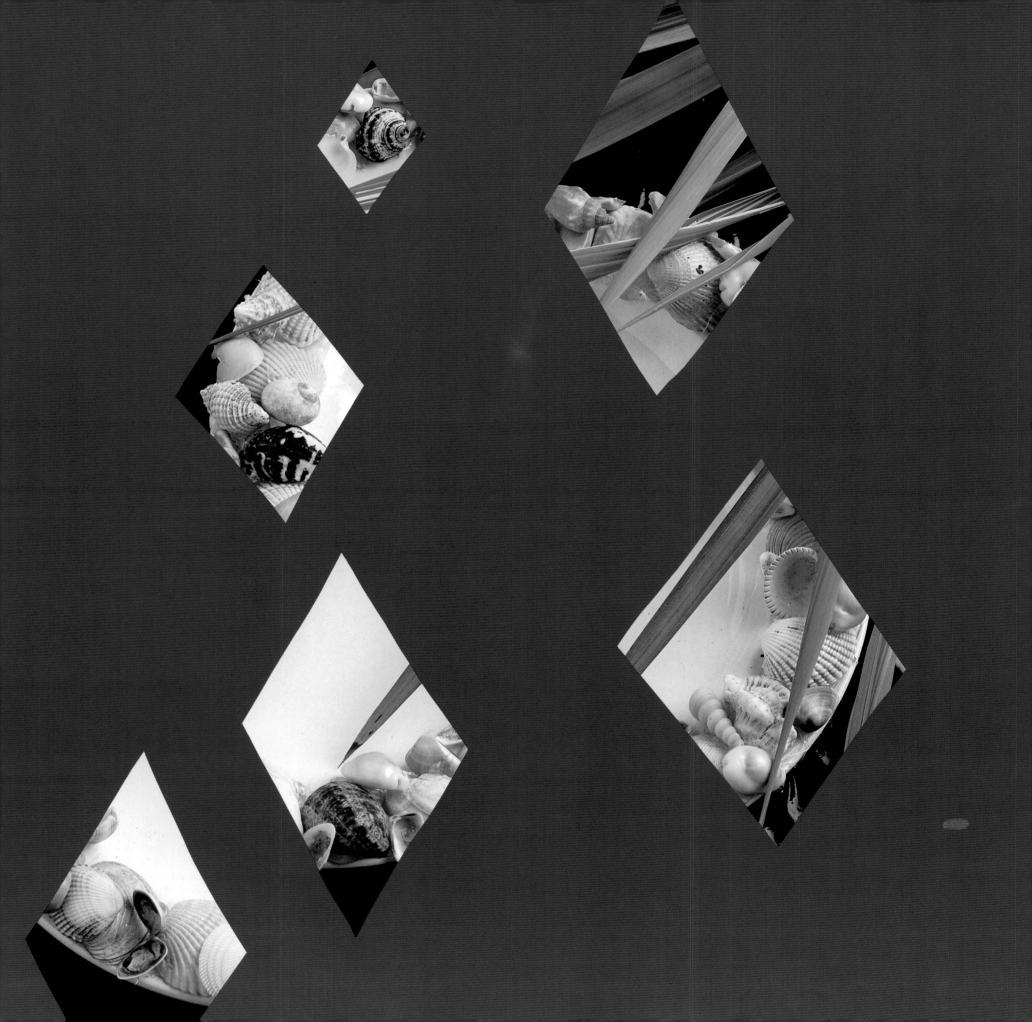

Whether it is embossed with a distinctive leaf vein pattern or a profusion of strawberries and vines, whether it has narrow ridges around the rim, or whether it is uncompromisingly plain, white tableware is the ultimate neutral colour. You can team it with crisp white table linen and decorate the table with contrasting trails of hops or ivy leaves; you can make a bold statement with bright scarlet napkins and deep red roses; or you can create an aura of sheer luxury by tucking milky-white orchids into each napkin.

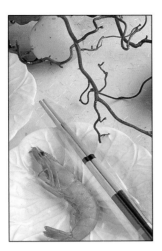

You can span several continents and incorporate white plates and dishes into a Japanese-style composition, or you can paint plain white plates with oriental motifs and team them with bamboo decorations of all kinds. When the guest list includes teenagers or younger children, you can maximize the starkness of white tableware by showing it off among all sorts of colourful and irresistible confections. These and many other decorative ideas in this section should prove that white tableware, in any setting, can be a positive design asset.

7 Wonderful White

RIGHT: The terracotta-coloured tablecloth, which tones with the pottery bowl, provides a sharp colour contrast to the crisp green and white scheme. Candles in holly green and natural rolled beeswax could be displayed in white or earthenware holders (instructions for making beeswax candles are given in Chapter 5). You can buy stiffened fabric bows from interior design shops.

Pool of Light

The cluster of white nightlights in a ring of ivy leaves and the deep green stiffened fabric bow on a crisp white napkin create an appealing colour contrast that looks well all the year round.

YOU WILL NEED

shallow earthenware or other
    pretty bowl
hot glue gun or clear, quick-
    setting glue
large ivy leaves
trails of variegated leaves
florist's scissors

1 Glue two overlapping layers of the large leaves around the inside of the bowl. Cover the base of the bowl with more leaves.

2 Glue trails of leaves to the outside of the bowl and glue on extra leaves if necessary to make the decoration look thick and green. Arrange the nightlights to fill the bowl.

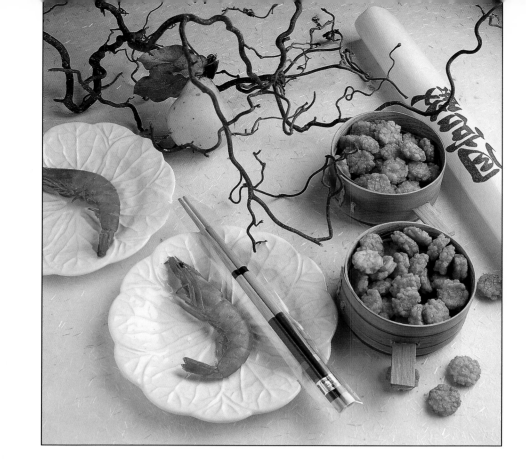

RIGHT: Cover the table with a sheet of Japanese drawing paper and stand a contorted twig in a marble pot or, if there is space, let it twist and twirl over the table, enhancing it by just one yellow golden quince. Fill small wooden rice steamers with rice crackers, set out the pointed-end chopsticks, and the meal can begin.

BELOW: Set the scene for a summer meal in the garden or indoors with trails of hops around the table, around the white pillar candles, over the napkins, everywhere. More hops cascade with palest pink everlasting pea from a textured white jug.

BELOW: It's a simple matter to glue tartan ribbon around a ring made of card and to stick a ribbon bow to one rim. This is an easy, but effective way of making napkin rings and smaller circles to hold a place setting of cutlery. The texture of the coarsely woven linen table napkin is exaggerated by the choice of table covering.

BELOW: Make someone's day with a breakfast tray set with pure white china and scarlet accessories. The napkin is held in a bone ring and the carefully selected strawberries have been set on scented geranium leaves.

ABOVE: White on white strikes a note of elegant simplicity. The cotton napkin, which has an embroidered decoration in one corner, is tied close to the centre point with three iris leaves, their ends cut slantwise. The single cream orchid, which has been tucked into the leaf band, could later be worn on a dress.

LEFT: You may not have gold-rimmed tableware or gold-plated cutlery, but do not let that stop you creating a gold-medal setting for a special occasion. The apple-shaped place mats have been cut from gold card, and there are small place cards to match. The finishing touches are twisted wire bows for napkin rings, black-edged ribbon around the cutlery and a glorious stiffened fabric bow as a table centrepiece.

Edge Shells

Transform unremarkable plates into ones with both texture and style by gluing shells around the rim and create individual shell sculptures for each place setting to set the scene for other seashore accessories.

YOU WILL NEED

inexpensive plates
hot glue gun or clear, quick-
    setting glue
selection of small shells

For the sculpture
selection of larger shells, such as
    oyster and cone shells

For the napkin holder
2 scallop shells, matched for size

For the cocktail sticks
selection of small shells, as
    varied as possible
wooden cocktail sticks or
    toothpicks

RIGHT: This black textured paper has a high gloss finish that makes it look like plastic. It makes a dramatic table covering for this seashore set, with the impressed pattern resembling ripples in the sand. The table decoration is simple and effective – a bunch of variegated grass leaves fanning out from a craggy shell.

1 To decorate each plate, glue small shells all around the rim, overlapping them so that the china is completely covered. Contrast neighbouring shells for shape, colour and texture.

2 To make a sculpture, select shells with a pleasing contrast of texture and shape. Choose a large flat shell, such as a scallop shell, as the background and glue others to it to make a fantasy shape.

ABOVE: Glue scallop shells together to make some stylish holders for paper napkins. Match the shells evenly for size and glue two together at the base. Place the holders at intervals around the table when you are serving finger foods such as unshelled prawns or asparagus.

ABOVE: Spearheading the latest in cocktail stick design, this set is made in moments. Simply glue pretty shells to wooden sticks and go off to mix the drinks.

RIGHT: A soft cream and green patterned cotton tablecloth captures the mood, whether it is for a summer party in the garden or a stylish wedding celebration. The napkin is held at the centre with a loop of cream paper ribbon, and the bow has been glued on top.

Ice-cool Cream

Cream and other pastel colours reflect the mood of summer. Here a medley of florist's and garden flowers have been arranged in a polished pewter bowl, and cream paper bows have been tied around cutlery and table napkins.

YOU WILL NEED

deep round or oval container
block of absorbent stem-holding
    foam, soaked in water
variegated foliage, such as
    pineapple mint
selection of pastel-coloured
    flowers, such as carnations,
    spray chrysanthemums,
    everlasting pea
florist's scissors

1 Arrange the foliage stems in the foam to create height and width all around the container and position others to fill in the centre.

2 Alternate the flower shapes and colours so that each contrasts well with its neighbours. Some flowers should slant low over the rim of the container.

3 Fill in the design with more flowers, still alternating the colours, and use more foliage stems to fill in any gaps.

Blue and white china has a long history. Most of the famous potteries have included exquisite examples of hand-painted willow pattern and other representational designs in their repertoires at one time or another, and food buffs declare that there is nothing like blue and white tableware – apart from plain white, perhaps – to show off food to advantage.

This section explores the design potential of tableware that, in the modern idiom, is spatter-painted blue on white, of pieces that simulate vibrant mosaics and of others that are sparsely decorated with a few strokes of the brush. It pays tribute to the translucence of fine bone china bowls, which can be used for finger bowls as well as for rice, and of the deepest blue Egyptian glass teamed, variously, with embossed white plates and with scarlet, pink and crimson woven straw fans. Whether the mood of the moment suggests a nautical theme by the use of woven cord place mats or accessories reflect the fireside glow of burnt-orange lilies, blue and white china will rise to the occasion.

8   Beautiful Blue

ABOVE: Blue and white tableware can be used to create any number of successful colour liaisons. Here the speckled plates have been set on a textured paper table covering and partnered with cotton napkins in a brighter shade of tan. Shiny cord, in two shades of the blue, has been knotted into a quick and easy napkin ring.

ABOVE: For a breakfast or late supper *à deux* a pretty hearts and flowers design has been stencilled with fabric paints on the textured cotton napkins. Rose-coloured cord has been used to tie the knot around the cutlery.

ABOVE: A place mat and napkin ring made of interwoven white cord and a tactile ring formed from two monkey's fist knots give a nautical look to a table set on denim blue hessian. Sunshine yellow spray chrysanthemums provide a sharp, almost acidic contrast to this setting, which would be as suitable for breakfast as for lunch.

LEFT: Lovely old plates with a central floral motif call for a hint of luxury in the choice of table accessories. The starched white napkins, ringed with gilt-edged ribbon bows and decorated with a cluster brooch and a full-blown rose, provide just that.

LEFT: The ingenious swan-shaped wooden place mats and coasters and the stylized wooden tulips require careful thought about the colours in the other table accessories. The problem is solved by drizzle-painting two used stone jars in blue and orange. A casual grouping of lilies echoes the informality of the mood. (Wooden items from Dansel Gallery)

Chequerboard

Glowing oyster-shell candles and coiled cord napkin rings contribute to the nautical theme in this crisp navy blue and white setting.

YOU WILL NEED

For the candles
lengths of wick
oyster shells
florist's adhesive clay or
    modelling clay
wooden cocktail sticks or
    toothpicks
ends of candles in chosen colour

For the napkin rings
white cord
cardboard tube
hot glue gun or clear, quick-
    setting glue
small shells

1 To make each candle cut a short length of wick and secure it to the inside of the oyster shell with a dab of adhesive clay. Tie the free end of the wick around the wooden stick so that the wick is held taut, and rest the stick on the shell.

2 Melt candle ends in a double boiler or a bowl over simmering water. Discard the pieces of wick and pour the wax into a small pan. Pour it into the shells and leave the wax to set. When it is set, melt some more wax and pour it into the shells to top up the hollows that will have formed. Trim the wick before lighting.

3 To make each napkin ring, wind the cord around the cardboard tube, pushing the strands close together. Bring one end of the cord diagonally over the band and glue it in place. Slip the completed ring off the cardboard tube. Trim the cord end to the required length and glue on a shell, which will be both decorative and will stop the end from fraying.

LEFT: Inexpensive blue glass plates have been partnered with white tableware to give an existing dinner set a fresh, new look. The check gingham napkins and even the candles combine the two colours and form a visual link between them.

LEFT: Take deep, dark blue plates, grapefruit glasses and candlesticks, set them on vibrant red, woven straw fans and you have a battle of the primaries. Candles striped from end to end with the two colours, a vase of deep crimson roses and a tablecloth ranging from green, through blue and mauve to red completes an extrovert scheme. (Glassware from The Pier)

LEFT: Tiny mosaic images depicting pieces of fruit and a two-coloured border will encourage you to be imaginative in your use of colour. You could set the plates on turquoise blue or orange woven place mats, decorate the table with blue or orange candles and provide table napkins in either of the principal hues. Alternatively, you could try a bold approach, and accentuate them both in a scheme that has both style and impact.

BELOW: Blue and white translucent china bowls make stylish finger bowls, especially when you are serving a Chinese meal. Half-fill the bowls with tepid water and float on the surface slices of lime or lemon, a spray chrysanthemum or a scattering of rose petals.

ABOVE: Blue glass plates and a scattering of glass marbles emphasize the blue floral pattern on the tableware, while stiffened fabric bows take up the theme. The fringed cotton gingham napkins and tablecloth reinforce the second colour element.

Pressed into Service

Pressed leaves, lawn daisies and primulas have been used to decorate brown eggshells to bring a note of sophistication to a springtime breakfast table, and a long-abandoned birds' nest makes a perfect container.

YOU WILL NEED

empty egg shells (see below)
a selection of pressed flowers
    and leaves
papercraft glue

1 To empty eggshells and leave them whole, use a darning needle to pierce a hole in each end. Hold the egg over a bowl and blow through one of the holes to release the egg white and yolk. Wash and dry the inside of the eggshell. Spread glue sparingly over the surface of the egg and press on the flowers and leaves. You can cover the eggs with flowers, position them in a random or polka-dot pattern or arrange the flowers and leaves to form a spray.

Tableware that has a many-coloured pattern has everything going for it. When it comes to teaming it with place mats or a tablecloth, with table napkins and a centrepiece decoration almost anything, in terms of colour, is possible. If you have a set of cups and saucers, dishes and bowls patterned with an Impressionist or botanical pattern of leaves and flowers, you can take your colour cue from any or all of the applied colours and then, the next meal around, completely change your approach.

You can set multi-coloured china on table coverings as diverse as blue net for a baptism celebration and glossy green wood for a summer garden party. You can bring together the individual colours featured in each piece of a coffee set by displaying it on any one of the vibrant colours or on a table cover that is a patchwork of all the hues. You can bring to life the floral pattern of a teaset by repeating the flower concept in a three-dimensional table arrangement or a leafy garland, or you can emphasize the many-coloured rings around uncompromisingly modern pottery with rings and loops of coloured beads around candles and napkins. Take stock of your multi-coloured tableware and count your blessings, for in design terms and in colour terms they are many and various.

9 Multi-coloured Marvels

RIGHT: Tableware with a many-coloured rim pattern seems by chance to be in sugared-almond colours. There are simple herb and flower posies in matching cups, and the gift pouches are piled into a bowl.

Birthday Celebration

Whether you choose the traditional blue-for-a-boy and pink-for-a-girl colours, or opt for a more varied approach, this pretty sugared-almond "tree" will enhance the setting for the birthday or baptism celebrations. The small net pouches of the sweetmeats are lucky take-home mementoes for your guests.

YOU WILL NEED

For the "Tree"
sugared almonds
preformed dry foam cone, 20cm/
    8in high
hot glue gun or clear, quick-
    setting glue
satin ribbons, 6mm/¼in wide
scissors
1 pin

For the Pouches
circles of coloured net, 15cm/6in
    in diameter
sugared almonds
satin ribbon, 6mm/¼in wide

1 To make the sugared-almond "tree", glue the sweets to the cone in rows or rings of each colour or in a random pattern.

2 Tie a small bow of satin ribbon and cut other lengths twice the height of the cone. Pin the bow to the centre of the ribbon lengths and pin it to the top of the decoration. Cut the ribbon ends slantwise.

3 To make the pouches place three or four sugared almonds in the centre of two net circles and tie them around the top with ribbon. It can look especially pretty if you use two different colours of net and use ribbons in a variety of colours.

RIGHT: Because the candle decorations use snippings and short-stemmed flowers, they can be a perfect match with the larger decorations in the room. A jug of rowan berries on a sideboard and small bowls of pansies at each place setting, for example, would complement the scarlet and mauve candle ring.

Candle Power

Creamy-white altar candles have been ringed around with flowers in soft, pastel shades and, on the right, in vibrant, contrasting hues. It is a decoration that can be composed in moments to take centre stage on a party table.

YOU WILL NEED

selection of short-stemmed
    plant materials, such as spray
    chrysanthemums, everlasting
    pea, pansies, marjoram, roses,
    lavender and verbena flowers,
    variegated pineapple mint
    foliage and rowan berries
white or cream straight-sided
    candles (we used candles that
    are 30cm/12in tall)
fine silver wire
florist's scissors
satin ribbon, 6mm/¼in wide

1 Cut the plant stems to equal lengths. Hold them against the candle and bind around them with silver wire. Add more and more stems until the floral hoop reaches all the way around the candle. Bind securely and fasten off the wire.

2 Wind a length of ribbon twice around the stems to cover the wire and tie it into a bow. Cut the ribbon ends slantwise.

ABOVE: A many-coloured bead bangle is a perfect match for this tissue-paper-edged papier mâché plate. Save discarded costume jewellery and look out for boxes of loose beads on market stalls and in charity shops so that you can thread them to match your tableware. It is a way of recycling with style.

ABOVE: Pottery decorated with brilliant bands of colour calls for lateral thinking when it comes to presentation. One of the colours is repeated in the table covering, another is picked up in the napkins, and they are all there in the bangles. The beads that encircle the candles and have been used for the napkin rings are threaded on to narrow leather thonging, which is simply tied in bows.

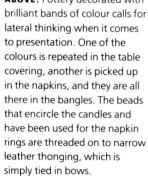

LEFT: If you have them, flaunt them! These black wooden plates, inlaid with mother-of-pearl, could be heirlooms or antique shop bargains. They have been set on a textured gold table covering to heighten the sheen factor, while the black napkins have been displayed with alternate bands, one of silver-embroidered braid and the other, a multi-strand bangle of pearl beads.

RIGHT: Treat collectors' plates to a touch of nostalgia. The deep pink border outlining a ring of holly sets this plate apart from the rest. It has been set on an old patchwork quilt covered with a lace-edged tablecloth, and the lacy table napkin is simply tied with a shot-silk ribbon bow.

BELOW: A Susie Cooper coffee set decorated in many colours is displayed on a Liberty wool cloth with a patchwork-like pattern. The vivid purple of the tray cloth and napkins exactly match one of the shades in the table covering.

LEFT: Sometimes, as here, the tableware has such a strong design that the setting needs little or no further embellishment. A blue woven tablecloth, blue and orange checked table napkins and a cluster of marigolds perfectly complement the art deco-style teaset.

Ring-a-Ring of Roses

When you are serving tea in the garden or displaying a cake for a special occasion what could be prettier than a garland of scented leaves and roses around the rim of the table? You can make a similar garland to drape across the vertical fall of a dining table or buffet table, or to hang around the dining room doorway.

YOU WILL NEED

coiled paper ribbon to tone with the foliage or flowers (you can use string or cord)
fine silver wire
variegated foliage, such as pineapple mint
roses
florist's scissors
hot glue gun, or clear, quick-setting glue
pins

1 Measure the garland core around the rim of the table or across the front, allowing a little extra to overlap. Tie the silver wire close to one end of the core and bind on the foliage, adding two or three stems at a time. Start by placing the tips of the sprays outwards and towards the ends of the core, so that the tips of each subsequent group cover the stem ends of the previous one. Continue binding on more foliage until the core is covered.

2 Glue the roses at intervals around the garland, alternating fully opened flowers with those in semi-bud. Spray the completed garland with water and keep it in a cool place until just before it is needed. Attach it to the tablecloth with pins.

Note: To keep the garland looking fresh and pretty for as long as possible, cut the foliage and flowers the day before you plan to use them, or at least several hours ahead, and leave them standing in water in a cool place.

ABOVE: A small, hand-arranged posy on each plate is a thoughtful, personal note for your guests. The fragrant stems of pineapple mint and dainty feverfew flowers have been tied with gossamer-fine ribbons streaked with pastel pink and green. (Ribbon by Offray)

LEFT: The exuberant floral pattern on the bone china teaset is echoed by the luxuriant floral garland around the rim of the table. (Tableware: Ophelia by Royal Albert)

RIGHT: Emphasize the ice-cool look by placing the frosted container on a glass plate and serving the dessert in chilled glass bowls. Glass serving spoons contribute to the glacier look.

Ice Cool Container

Capture the everlasting beauty of colourful flowers or petals by setting them in a wall of ice. When it is frozen, the ice bowl is a really cool container for sorbet, ice cream and other chilled desserts.

YOU WILL NEED

2 bowls of similar shape and
    different sizes
water
heavy weight
selection of edible flowers and
    leaf sprays, such as pansies,
    feverfew, clary and pineapple
    mint
florist's scissors
wooden skewer
aluminium foil

1 Place one bowl inside the other. Pour water into the gap between the two bowls and place the weight inside the top one so that the water is pushed up level with the rims. Insert flowers all around the bowl.

2 Use a wooden skewer to arrange the flowers and to push some of them underneath the top bowl. You will need to pack the flowers and leaves quite closely to prevent some of them from floating to the top. Cover the bowl with foil and freeze it. Run a little hot water around the bowls to release the ice decoration. Wrap it in foil and keep it in the freezer until just before it is needed.

Acknowledgements

t = top   b = bottom   r = right   l = left

Page 15(b) Cupola Nera by Rosenthal Studio House Ltd; p16 Arco White by Villeroy & Boch; p24(b) Curzon by Wedgwood; p27 Tableware from The Pier; p34 Candle by the Melford Candle Company; p35(b) Fish-patterned pottery from Evans Kitchen Shop; p38 Tableware from The Pier; p42 Cairo by Rosenthal House Ltd; p45 Strawberry and Vine china by Wedgwood; p46 Vie Sauvage by Villeroy & Boch; p58(r) Tableware by Royal Doulton; p59(bl) Vase from The Pier; p63 Pottery from Evans Kitchen Shop; p64 Ribbon by V.V. Rouleaux; p75(t) Papier mâché items by Alison Hay; p78 Beeswax candle kit from Easy-Bee Candles; p87(tl) Tableware from The Pier; p89 Malvern by Royal Doulton; p100(bl) Tableware from The Pier; p101(tl) Tableware from The Pier; p109 Wooden items from Damsel Gallery; p112 Glassware from The Pier. The Publishers and author are also grateful to the following manufacturers and retailers for the loan of tableware and accessories: C.M. Offray, Ashford, Middx (for ribbons) Paperchase, London (for paper tableware and novelties) Price's Patent Co Ltd, London (for candles)